Cars
We Loved in the
1970s

Cars
We Loved in the
1970s

Giles Chapman

The
History
Press

First published 2013

The History Press
The Mill, Brimscombe Port
Stroud, Gloucestershire, GL5 2QG
www.thehistorypress.co.uk

British Library Cataloguing in Publication Data.
A catalogue record for this book is available from
the British Library.

ISBN 978 0 7524 9432 6

Typesetting and origination by The History Press
Printed in India

INTRODUCTION

On the one hand, you had hatchbacks, superminis, electronics and turbochargers – design and technology that would shape the cars we drive in the twenty-first century. On the other, most of the bestsellers were decidedly old fashioned, with drive to the rear wheels, sophisticated rear suspension a rarity, and styling that was a throwback to Detroit *c.* 1967. The 1970s could be a strange time for cars.

No two mid-1970s models make a clearer contrast than the Austin Allegro and the Honda Accord. The former was simply not up to scratch, despite its manufacturer's vast experience, while the latter was great to drive and beautifully built from a company tiptoeing into the family car arena for the first time.

The old order was changing, and so was the motoring environment. Roads were faster but traffic was growing. Cars were safer but, with fuel supplies almost constantly in chaos, the cost of running them was going through the roof. Still, there was the incredible Lamborghini Countach to fantasise about. And you could always rely on a Little Chef for food, the AA's Relay service to get you home, and a hovercraft to whisk you off to Europe in double-quick time.

This book takes you straight back to the 1970s, profiles fifty of the best-loved cars of the era and relives life on Britain's roads in all its variety. Indeed, we so wanted to make it authentic that our parade of '70s motors actually begins in the late 1960s, where important models – the Jaguar XJ6, the Volvo 145 – making their debut would become synonymous with the decade ahead. Likewise, little from 1978/79 changed the roadscape so we've squeezed cars that mostly found fame in the '80s into a chapter of their own.

And all of it is enhanced with the most evocative images of the period that we could lay our hands on. Fasten your seatbelt – or not – and enjoy the drive back in time.

Saab 99, 1967

You'd have been a rational and clued-up driver to choose the Saab 99 when it arrived in Britain in the autumn of 1969.

Previous Saabs had been powered by two-stroke engines, but this all-new, larger car offered a four-stroke, four-cylinder motor made for the Swedish company by Triumph. It was a 'slant-four' unit, leaning over by 45 degrees, to lower the 99's centre of gravity and its bonnet height. With a capacity of 1709cc, it powered the front wheels and, uniquely, had the clutch at the front and the gearbox tucked underneath. This compact, low-mounted drivetrain, plus double-wishbone front suspension, endowed the 99 with polished handling and roadholding.

You could tell this car was developed for the tough Nordic environment. It had an electric cooling fan when such things were unheard of, four-wheel disc brakes, a deep wraparound windscreen, and an ignition key position between the front seats to lock the car's transmission when parked.

To enhance this impressive roster, by 1974 Saab had given the 99 four

The original Saab 99, a tough Swedish car jam-packed with safety innovations.

world-first safety features: headlamp wipers and washers; bumpers that sprang back into shape after a 5mph bash; side impact protection beams in the doors; and a glass-fibre headlining to protect occupants if the car overturned. Along the way, it also introduced the motoring world to its first heated driver's seat.

From 1977, the 99 also became an unlikely but very capable performance car when fitted with a turbocharger. But for the first half of the '70s, it was simply the safest, most sophisticated family car around.

WHO LOVED iT?

The thinking driver's choice, and not that much more costly than equivalent 'ordinary' cars, 99s were bought by early adopter professionals like architects and doctors.

In 1974, Saab added a hatchback option to the 99 and named it the Combi Coupé.

WHAT THEY SAID AT THE TIME

'The body's very low drag and really roomy accommodation confirm that Saab got their priorities right, regardless of what you think of the aesthetics.' – *Motor* magazine in November 1969 on the £1,294 99 two-door.

Jaguar XJ6, 1968

Hmmm, something seemed oddly awry with the judgement of the 1969 European Car of the Year awards panel. Jaguar's XJ6 was manifestly a truly exceptional motor car, and yet the good burghers of COTY gave the trophy to the deadly dull, if worthy, Peugeot 504. *Car* magazine, for one, attempted to redress the balance with its own gong, and by simply stating: 'It makes redundant all cars that cost more.'

And why was it so great? Well, not for being particularly novel. It was a conventional, large, four-door, four-seater saloon with coil-spring suspension, a front engine and rear-wheel drive – nothing like as radical as, say, the rotary-engined NSU Ro80.

But Jaguar's engineers, led by suspension genius Bob Knight, masterfully fine-tuned the whole car to combine ride comfort and silence with handling and roadholding – qualities previously thought irreconcilable in a luxury car. Partly thanks to its plump tyres, specially designed by Dunlop, the XJ6 was more nimble even than Jaguar's own E-type and yet eclipsed the Rolls-Royce Silver Shadow for its composure of ride.

Special, plump tyres were just one ingredient of the XJ6's magic carpet ride.

Like all Jags, the XJ6 was a visual treat; low, feline and aggressive but elegant as well. And the interior, from its walnut facia to the individually sculpted rear seats, was utterly alluring.

Under the broad bonnet lived Jaguar's XK engine in 2.8-, 3.4- and 4.2-litre sizes (a stunning V12 engine arrived in 1972 in the similar XJ12), fed with petrol from twin fuel tanks.

The XJ6 was a bargain, often undercutting comparable Mercedes-Benz models by 50 per cent, and this style of XJ6 was on sale until 1987.

WHO LOVED iT?

A lengthy waiting list formed immediately, causing one delegation of Swiss buyers to complain en masse. However, increasingly patchy build quality saw many Brits defect to German luxury cars, meaning mid-1970s buyers often had to be arch patriots. Nevertheless, new boss John Egan rejuvenated both company and car in the 1980s.

The lean and slinky lines of the XJ6 were recognisably Jaguar yet also deftly modern.

Volvo 144 & 145, 1968

These robust and conservative Swedish cars spoke volumes about their buyers' tastes and aspirations; they were reassuringly expensive but never brash, and were seemingly custom-made for taking children back to boarding school, or the Labradors out for a run on the heath.

And, indeed, Britain's middle classes should have been congratulated for buying wisely. The 144 saloon and its 145 estate brother, launched in 1968, drew on all the rugged attributes of previous Volvos but in a smart new style for the 1970s, and with a continuing focus on safety.

The front and rear sections had energy-absorbing, in-built crumple zones and the steering column was collapsible. The car's braking was split on a triangular pattern, guaranteeing 80 per cent of braking capability for the driver even if the system failed. More safety innovations followed later, including three world firsts as standard: rear seatbelts; front seat head restraints; and rear door child locks.

This is the GL edition of the 144 saloon, considerably less sluggish thanks to fuel injection.

Nonetheless, all 140-type Volvos felt heavy and sluggish until the arrival of fuel injection for the 2-litre on GL versions in 1971.

By 1973, the cars sprouted prominent rubber-faced bumpers and a padded steering wheel to keep ahead of US safety laws and further satisfy safety-conscious buyers, although this was but a prelude to the dodgem car looks of the replacement 240 range in 1974. Direct descendants of the 144, moreover, would be on sale for twenty-seven years.

WHAT THEY SAID AT THE TIME

'As an estate car it must offer all that anyone could want in terms of useable space; it is plenty big enough for sleeping in too, but a bit large for parking.' – *Motor* magazine in June 1969 on the £1,580 Volvo 145.

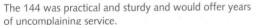

The 144 was practical and sturdy and would offer years of uncomplaining service.

The 145 estate, darling of Britain's antiques dealers during the 1970s.

WHO LOVED iT?

BBC1's *The Good Life* made the point about these big, safe and solid Volvos so perfectly. Corporate suburbanite Jerry Leadbetter was smugly proud of his yellow 145 estate, as it purred along the leafy avenues of Surbiton. And so were thousands of like-minded real people.

Fiat 128, 1969

Fiat churned out over 3 million of these little saloons and yet the 128 is a car that's almost completely forgotten today. It's an undeserved fate, really, because the 128 was the first Fiat with the familiar modern layout; it's front-wheel drive with a transversely mounted engine. The engine itself was an all-new overhead-camshaft design in 1100 and 1300cc versions, with its four-speed gearbox mounted behind it, while the supple suspension system consisted of MacPherson struts at the front and transverse leaf springs behind. Front disc brakes were standard, too.

So it was certainly a surefooted and lively thing, and one that could give you 40mpg fuel economy very easily. Apart from the flimsy controls and stark interior, it would still drive fairly well – if noisily – by today's standards, and it was a deserved European Car of the Year in 1970.

The 128 had two downsides. The first was soon glaringly obvious as the 1970s wore on. Its lack of a hatchback put it at a major disadvantage against the new breed of superminis like the

Italy's equivalent to the Austin 1100, the Fiat 128 did quite well in Britain … at first.

Renault 5 and Fiat's own 127. The other problem was shadier: the 128 was uncommonly rust-prone, disintegrating like a wind-fallen apple in a muggy orchard.

The styling of the 128 in two- or four-door saloon or two-door estate forms was plain, if not downright boring, but there were a couple of sporty derivatives in the 128 Coupé and the 3P, a fastback with a tailgate, that were undoubted lookers.

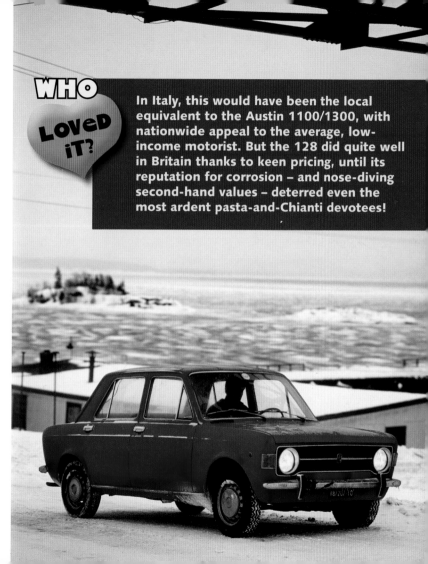

WHO LOVED iT?

In Italy, this would have been the local equivalent to the Austin 1100/1300, with nationwide appeal to the average, low-income motorist. But the 128 did quite well in Britain thanks to keen pricing, until its reputation for corrosion – and nose-diving second-hand values – deterred even the most ardent pasta-and-Chianti devotees!

WHAT THEY SAID AT THE TIME

'In our opinion, this is another Fiat winner. The 128 is a good all-rounder which does most things well, some very well, few badly.' – *Motor* magazine in April 1970 on the £875 Fiat 128 four-door.

Snowy roads covered with salt – not too good for the 128's rust-prone metalwork.

Ford Capri MkI, 1969

Ford took the bold decision to try to repeat the magic trick of the American Ford Mustang in a European context, and drafted in several of the designers who created the first 'personal car' to assist. Just as with the Mustang, the Capri aimed to bring an affordable and reliable product to those who longed for a sports car but couldn't afford one, or

The original Capri was a sports car for commuters; note the side air intakes, entirely sham ones!

else knew how impractical it would be for everyday driving. The original Mustang had drawn heavily on the Ford Falcon, and the Capri – launched to great fanfare in early 1969 – would derive all of its mechanical hardware from the mechanically simple Escort and Cortina.

Besides the long bonnet/short fastback styling, with those distinctive 'hockey stick' mouldings and racing car-style air intakes along its sides, the Capri scored by offering a mind-boggling mix-and-match of engines,

trim levels and liveries. So you could pretty much create your own car with anything from a 1.3-litre four-cylinder to a 3-litre V6 engine, and then jazz it up as sportily or luxuriously as your imagination – or wallet – allowed.

The typical Capri was a 1.6 that, with a tailwind, was just about a 100mph machine. Unlike an exotic Alfa Romeo or Lancia, it could take any amount of daily abuse, and had the benefit of being a proper four-seater beneath those rakish lines. Unlike an Italian sports car, racing

wasn't really in the blood. For a Capri to win races, it had to either have a trick engine or be a proper racing car with a Capri-shaped body. But that didn't stop a million people buying a MkI by 1973.

WHAT THEY SAID AT THE TIME

'[They] surprised us by their astonishing quietness and refinement, and by the excellence in both cars of the gear change, as well as the clutch and throttle action. In all these departments, this brace of Fords put to shame a so-called "thoroughbred" Italian car that we had on test at the same time.' – *Motor* magazine in August 1969 on the £1,065 Capri 1300GT XLR and the £1,167 Capri 2000GT XLR.

Crazy paving, c-ray-zee guy: Ford went big on individualising each Capri for its owner.

WHO LOVED IT?

Well, everyone, it seemed, or at least most young men with a spark of jack-the-lad to them, and then quite a lot of their dads. Indeed, with its four seats and cheap-to-run nature, a Capri was actually quite a sensible choice for the married chap newly in the family way. The aura of *The Professionals*, *Minder* and *Only Fools & Horses* descended much later.

15

Mini Clubman, 1969

If ever there was a car that symbolised motoring Britain in the 1960s then it was the brilliant Mini. A full ten years after its launch, it was still selling very strongly, and had even become a marque in its own right, with the former Austin and Morris prefixes dropped.

The company producing the car, British Leyland, nevertheless realised there was an urgent need to update its smallest product. It knew rivals had taken the Mini's pace-setting packaging – making more room for passengers thanks to compact front-wheel drive and a transversely mounted engine – and would soon feature it in more comfortable modern cars.

The new Mini Clubman, unveiled in 1969 and in showrooms by 1970, was British Leyland's answer. Slightly weirdly, the company had altered the Mini's most distinctive feature, its rounded, cheeky visage, by substituting an entirely new square nose section that gave it the anonymous style of a Hillman Hunter – and pointlessly added 4.5in to the car's length.

Much more worthwhile was the interior. The most obvious change was the instrument pack, now mounted in an oblong box ahead of the driver, and visible through a new three-spoke steering wheel. For the first time there were fresh air vents. Seats were reshaped, re-trimmed and

The greatest invention since the wheel.

A 1971 ad for the Clubman. How did they slip that claim past the Advertising Standards Authority?

WHO LOVED iT?

From the start, the Mini had universal, classless appeal. The Clubman – looks, perhaps, apart – slightly enhanced its comfort and style. Still, it probably had most appeal to the Mini's core customers who craved a better driving environment and less wearying mechanical racket.

given a stitched pattern, new door trim panels were a feature, and – best of all – the car was much quieter thanks to extra sound-insulation material and a new moulded carpet set. Like all post-'69 Minis, it had wind-down windows instead of sliding ones, meaning the famous door bins were dropped.

A sister car was the Mini 1275GT, with a 1275cc engine, go-faster stripes and front disc brakes – it was the Clubman-style equivalent to a Cooper. And the standard Clubman saloon and estate also saw a power boost in 1975, with a larger 1098cc engine.

It was, in the main, a decently improved Mini, and it helped push the range to its best-ever sales year in 1971, a huge 318,475 cars. But the Clubman was dropped in 1980 when the Austin Mini-Metro arrived … and the standard-shaped Mini outlived it by a further twenty years!

'A dramatic overall improvement in both creature comforts and drivability. No longer is a long Mini journey something of an endurance test.' – *Motor* magazine in October 1969 on the £720 Mini Clubman.

An entirely misleading idea of how cumbersome items will fit into a Clubman's boot. Notice the Denovo run-flat wheels/tyres.

The 1973 Mini saloon line-up, left to right: 1275GT, 1000, Clubman.

17

Citroën GS, 1970

The GS filled the wide gap in Citroën's range between the humble Dyane and Ami at one end and the glamorous DS at the other. The aerodynamic fastback body style was immediately Citroën-esque and daringly modern. But its specification was a fascinating cocktail of iconic features from both extremes of the Citroën spectrum.

Like the 2CV and the Dyane, the GS featured a horizontally opposed, air-cooled engine, albeit an all-new unit with four cylinders instead of two, driving its front wheels. But like the DS, its sleek lines encased hydropneumatic suspension and all round disc brakes. The ride height was adjustable so the car could negotiate rutted tracks or hunker down for motorway cruising.

The hugely roomy interior featured squashy seats and, like the DS, a single-spoke steering wheel. Relatively meagre luggage accommodation (there was no hatchback until the modified GSA arrived in 1979) was compensated for by the capacious GS estate introduced in 1972, and levels of trim ranged from the basic Confort to the leather-rich Pallas.

Maybe a touch underpowered, with a 1-litre engine expected to

There was widespread amazement at the high-tech/low-price achievement of the GS; this is a mildly sporty GSX2.

haul along a relatively heavy car, there was an engine upgrade to 1.2-litre in 1973. Still no firecracker, the GS remained a spacious, economical family car with an exceptionally smooth ride and fantastic roadholding. Most of all, it extended Citroën choice into the mainstream sector with a car that was adventurous in design. The GS was a multi-faceted thing bound to inspire pride in any technologically minded owner, even if that made it something of a scary prospect as a used car purchase.

WHO LOVED iT?

The GS was the Chevrolet Volt or Nissan Leaf of its time, bristling with interesting technological features yet aimed at those who perhaps valued comfort and economy above outright performance. It was a huge seller, with 2.5 million made.

WHAT THEY SAID AT THE TIME

'Every aspect of its design and behaviour demands superlatives. But the really astonishing thing is that such a technologically advanced car can be produced at such a low price.' – *Car* magazine in March 1971 on the £1,001 GS.

The Break was the estate version of the GS, best placed to exploit its amazing ride quality.

Datsun Cherry 100A, 1970

Time to meet one of Britain's true motoring pioneers. Yes, that's right, Britain's: the little Cherry was the first Japanese car to see mainstream volume sales success in this country. Indeed, by 1974 Datsun could claim it was the biggest-selling single imported car model. Toyota may have been larger than Datsun globally but the Cherry helped to make Datsun Japan's most successful importer here, and began to pave the way for the momentous Datsun/Nissan decision to build a factory at Sunderland.

So what kind of car was this ground-breaker? Well, by the cautious and conventional Japanese engineering standards of the day, really quite a good one. The Cherry was only the second car from Japan to feature a transverse engine driving the front wheels (the first being the tiny Honda N360/600). To the surefootedness of this set-up Datsun brought its typically light clutch and steering, a fairly competent all-independent suspension system, and front disc brakes.

The 1-litre four-cylinder engine allowed entirely adequate service for economical motoring with its 59bhp. Its mechanical excellence, general refinement and dependability certainly endeared it to anyone who bought one.

There was, however, no hatchback despite the slightly tinny-looking styling of the two- and four-door saloons, although there was a small two-door estate, and the Cherry 120A Coupé did come with a tailgate (and a very high sill)

Datsun's Cherry 100A was the Japanese marque's first transverse-engined, front-wheel-drive car.

Weird styling and terrible rear visibility in the nonetheless capacious 100A Coupé.

plus the mildly added zest of a 1.2-litre motor. Interiors felt plasticky and tacky compared to European rivals. Europeans may have scoffed at first, but the Cherry certainly was a credible competitor to such upcoming greats as the Fiat 127 and Renault 5.

How long will you feel like this about your next new car?

Some carmakers get fashion models to promote their wares; Datsun chose Hattie Jacques.

WHO LOVED iT?

British buyers gravitated towards the Cherry (and especially the later Sunny 120Y) because of competitive pricing, a good spec of equipment, and because they were easy to drive and were reliable. This tended to foster good relations with dealers, the word spread, and sales rocketed ... to the alarm of British Leyland.

Ford Cortina MkIII 1970

The Cortina in MkII guise topped the sales charts in 1967 and invariably hogged the No 2 position during the rest of the 1960s. For the car's third incarnation, Ford of Europe decided the Cortina and Germany's Ford Taunus would be replaced with one car, and formed an Anglo-German design team to evolve it. By October 1970, it was ready to be unveiled.

The Cortina MkIII in 2000XL, being greeted here by an Escort MkI, another massively popular Ford.

While the MkI and MkII Cortinas had been basically similar under the skin, the MkIII was totally new, with only the basically unaltered 1.3- and 1.6-litre engines carried over. There would be no Lotus edition, but there was a powerful 2-litre engine and a natty-looking GT.

The 168in length was actually the same as the MkII's but you'd never guess it, thanks to a 3.5in longer wheelbase, 2.1in width increase, a 3.5in wider front track and 5in wider rear track, and a 2.7in drop in height. The most distinctive styling feature,

however, was the undulating wing-line contour, often referred to as the 'Coke bottle' shape or, according to one Ford designer, 'a hop-up feature'. It looked pretty nifty in metallic paint.

More practically, the boot lid now opened down to bumper level, pointed front-wing tips made precise manoeuvres easier, and the fuel filler was concealed behind a metal flap. Rack-and-pinion steering was a vast improvement, and new all-round coil-spring suspension, supported by upper and lower wishbones, boosted comfort and refinement.

Slightly higher prices put no brake on demand. After six years on sale, 1.2 million were sold. Britain's deep trust of the Cortina brand, together with feeble opposition, returned the MkIII to the sales charts pinnacle in 1972.

WHAT THEY SAID AT THE TIME

'The car has a strong sporting bias. It has a top speed of over 100mph, impressive acceleration, an excellent gearbox and gear change, light positive steering, good roadholding and roll-free cornering that encourages brisk motoring.' – *Motor* magazine in October 1970 on the £1,338 Cortina 2000 GXL.

Here is the Cortina MkIII GT looking slick with its coach line and Rostyle fake alloy wheels.

WHO LOVED iT?

As Britain's bestseller for four whole years, it seemed anyone and everyone was a potential Cortina buyer, such was the huge choice of body style, equipment and engine. But its popularity was hugely boosted by fleet sales, as a company car started to become an expected perk in the white-collar business world.

Hillman Avenger, 1970

The Hillman Avenger was something actually quite rare in the car industry, even today: it was brand new from nose to tail. However, in stark contrast to the design dynamism and creative engineering of the Citroën GS that year, the Avenger was completely lacking in innovation. With its rear-wheel drive via a coil-spring-suspended beam rear axle, the Avenger was as utterly conventional and conservative as the Ford Escort and Vauxhall Viva against which its manufacturer, the Rootes Group, was pitching it.

The considerable upside was that it was thoroughly contemporary in the looks department, with the crisp, undulating lines scaled down to a British size from contemporary American sedans. The Avenger was handsome as a two- or four-door saloon or five-door estate. The range of newly developed 1250 and 1500cc overhead-valve engines (uprated to 1300cc and 1600cc in 1974) made for sturdy workhorses, while rack-and-pinion steering helped towards predictable road manners. Unusual plastic cylindrical controls on the steering column worked the wipers and lights.

The only pulse-raiser was the rare and short-lived 1972–73 Avenger Tiger, with twin carbs, 107bhp, brash boy-racer war paint and tail spoiler. Having said that, the 75bhp 1.5-litre Avenger GT was a reasonably peppy motor, too.

Rootes got the Avenger pretty well spot on for the British market of the time. It was tough, easy to live with and simple to service at home – this last was a key purchase decider at a time when people could still adjust their own engines. It became the Chrysler Avenger in 1976 and the Talbot Avenger in 1980, and even enjoyed a short stint on sale in the USA as the Plymouth Cricket.

The Avenger was a well-judged entrant to the core 1970s family car market. Anyone here intending to drive home?

This copper-coloured Avenger is photographed in Malta, where the car was launched to the largely approving motoring press.

WHO LOVED iT?

Rootes had been selling the ultra-conservative Hillman Minx range for years, and the Avenger was a natural progression for many Minx owners. The car also made ever more sense throughout the early 1970s as buyers of Morris Marinas and Austin Allegros discovered the fundamental shortcomings of these cars.

A ghosted technical image of the Avenger, showing its ultra-conventional layout, beloved of DIYers.

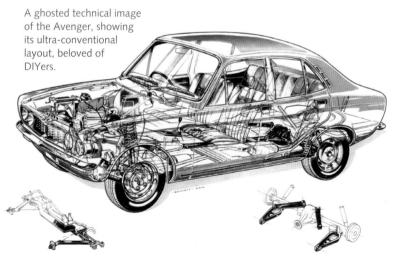

WHAT THEY SAID AT THE TIME

'Roomy but compact small family saloon, conventional in design; generally quiet, refined and comfortable; very good roadholding and handling; reasonable performance and economy.' – *Motor* magazine in February 1970 on the £903 Avenger GL.

25

Life on the Road in 1970s Britain

For a short but golden period between 1959, when the M1 opened, and 1965, Britain's drivers had been able to explore the full performance potential of their cars without restraint. There was no upper speed limit. If you owned a Jaguar E-type and you wanted to see if it really could attain the 150mph top speed its manufacturer claimed (it couldn't, incidentally), you could find out on the public highway rather than at a race circuit.

In 1965, however, the high-speed free-for-all stopped abruptly when a 70mph motorway limit was introduced. Touted at the time as an experiment, on 22 December it was made permanent and it has never been lifted. Performance car drivers have agitated and railed against it ever since.

➤ No wonder this stretch of 1970s M4 motorway looks so empty; we're heading east and still haven't got to Cardiff yet …

◄ Traffic in London in the mid-1970s, at Portland Place. Things never change: moving at a snail's pace, nowhere to park, and traffic wardens ready to pounce!

▲ Britain's roads were gradually filling up, as the country's 'vehicle parc' rose from 15 to 19 million through the decade.

◄ The M4 coming into London in around 1975, where drivers had to use the North or South Circular Roads to avoid fighting their way through the centre of the city; construction of the M25 had barely begun.

Still, it was probably a good thing. By 1970, the number of vehicles on the UK's roads had swelled to some 15 million, and showed no signs of levelling off. Cutting road casualties was an absolute priority. In that year, 7,499 people were killed on the nation's road network, with a further 356,000 injured. Clamping down on speed was just one of the ways in which drivers needed 'taming'.

The motorway-building programme of the 1960s had vastly reduced journey times. The M2, M3, M4, M5, M6 and M62 were already largely in place, with the completion of the M5 between Birmingham and Bristol, and the M6 from Birmingham to the Scottish border, in 1970 meaning that the network was now over 1,000 miles long. Its tentacles stretched to most parts of England, and distances between major cities really seemed to have shrunk.

Through the 1970s, the emphasis switched to dual carriageways, led by the widened, vastly improved A1, and dozens of towns that had become choked with traffic got bypasses. The A64 York Bypass that opened in 1975 was a prime example of the traffic relief that such schemes could bring to historic cities. Motorway-building, though, continued too. In 1971, the M6 through Birmingham was opened and was linked up to the M5, and three years later the M5 itself was extended by the opening of the Avon Bridge. In 1976 the east–west M62 joined Liverpool and Hull, and, all the while, laborious progress was being made on the M25, with five sections completed by 1977; it wouldn't be totally navigable until 1986.

▲ Backed-up traffic crawls into a contraflow on a motorway in about 1976, the start of Britain's antipathy for these highways that once promised high-speed freedom.

Many rural A-roads like this meandered through small towns and villages, leading to a 1970s boom in building bypasses.

Having the motorways there was one thing; being able to exploit their full potential was another, in the face of world events.

After the Arab-Israeli 'Yom Kippur' war in October 1973, Britain's politicians got the jitters about oil supplies. Saving fuel became a new mantra, and the first move towards that was to print millions of books of petrol rationing coupons in November 1973 to limit consumption. Although the scheme was kept on standby, the government took a different tack on 8 December by introducing a blanket 50mph national speed limit. The aim was to economise by saving £700 million in oil imports as prices had spiralled five-fold thanks to the Arab oil embargo. This driving misery was enforced with speed traps, unmarked police patrol cars and the maximum speeding fine doubled to £100. You had to be extremely vigilant at the wheel, too, because the road signs weren't amended.

The limits had been lifted by May 1974 but then, from 15 December that year, energy-saving rules were imposed again, this time pegging the

▲ Britain was badly hit by the 1973 Arab oil embargo, but North Sea drilling rigs like this one, BP's Sea Quest pictured in 1972, would soon begin piping black gold to British shores, leading to a period of oil self-sufficiency for the UK.

top whack on unrestricted single-carriageway roads at 50mph and on dual carriageways at 60mph; they were in force until May 1977, when 60mph and 70mph respectively were reinstated.

Organisations like the Royal Society for the Prevention of Accidents (RoSPA) wouldn't be found complaining about the cuts in speed, but throughout the decade its emphasis was on teaching people to use roads more carefully. In 1971, for example, it launched the Green Cross Code, using research from the Transport & Road Research Laboratory to comprehensively improve on the stern and dictatorial Kerb Drill. The new Code was much more accommodating of children's actual capabilities, for example showing them *where* to cross a busy street and not just *how*, and also introduced a towering Green Cross Code Man character to front campaigns and publicity tours. This was played by Dave Prowse, later to animate Darth Vader in the *Star Wars* movies. Also in 1971, RoSPA employed bike star Barry Sheene to get the safety message

▲ A panicky UK government had millions of these petrol rationing coupons printed, but the scheme barely got off the ground and was replaced by one built around a blanket 50mph national speed limit.

over to motorcyclists. In 1976, meanwhile, the spotlight wax turned on equestrians, as RoSPA and the British Horse Society collaborated to design a road safety test for riders, in a bid to cut the 3,000 on-highway horse-related mishaps that occurred annually.

Every new car sold in the UK since April 1961 had had front seatbelts fitted as standard, but drivers showed an astonishing reluctance to wear

▲ This crash-test rig at Vauxhall's Luton engineering centre is being readied for a Chevette impact test in 1976. The crash-test dummy is belted in – unlike the vast majority of real drivers at the time.

▲ A 1976 report demanded a redoubled crackdown on drink-drivers, with the breathalyser the chosen method of detection; its recommendations took seven years to become law.

▲ Work on the Channel Tunnel came to a grinding halt in 1975, leaving the hovercraft as the quickest and most high-tech method of getting to mainland Europe for drivers.

them. In June 1973 it was found only 27 per cent routinely buckled up, and the government splashed out a then huge £850,000 on its 'Clunk-click – every trip' ad campaign to try to change attitudes. However, it seemed that only legislation would make any real difference and in 1974 ministers got the ball rolling against a national chorus of 'Nanny State' protest cries. Nevertheless, it would take eleven attempts and nine years to make wearing front belts mandatory, and that was despite Formula 1 star Jackie Stewart imploring MPs to get on with it in a speech in the House of Commons in 1978.

Despite the introduction of the breathalyser for those suspected of driving while under the influence of alcohol, the government felt a new impetus was needed in the fight against drink-driving. Frank Blennerhassett QC was tasked with thoroughly investigating the situation, and his report published in 1976, after two years' work, recommended streamlining test procedures so that boozed-up miscreants couldn't wriggle free of convictions on technicalities; making breath-testing the norm rather than blood tests; targeting high-risk offenders; allowing the police discretionary powers to test; and redoubling efforts on publicity campaigns. Most of the advice passed into law in 1983, with significant reductions in drink-driving subsequently.

Ever since 1957, when the first roll-on/roll-off car ferry route was introduced between Tilbury and Antwerp, driving to the Continent had been getting easier and easier. There was no longer a need to have your car craned on and off a ship, and although cross-Channel hovercraft services arrived in 1968, the last of the cars-by-air services from British Air Ferries closed down in 1974.

Getting to Europe under the sea was thought to be the route of the future. But although a start on a tunnel was made on both the British and French sides in 1973, the work ground to a halt in 1975 as the cash-strapped British government decided to axe the funding. The wait for completion would be a long one indeed, the first passengers not able to travel through the finished Channel Tunnel until 1994.

What else happened on Britain's roads in the 1970s? Well, the first 'sleeping policemen' speed inhibitors were experimentally laid in 1975, which was the same year that hand signals were finally dropped from the driving test. And London got its first bus lane, in gridlocked Wandsworth, in 1977. The following year, the Highway Code included the Green Cross Code for pedestrians, the orange badge scheme for the disabled and, in the face of soaring vehicle crime, advice on vehicle security, all for the first time.

But perhaps most importantly of all, by 1980 the yearly death toll on the nation's highways had fallen to 5,953, with injuries cut to 323,000. With the number of vehicles swelling simultaneously to 19 million, that was really quite an achievement.

Toyota Carina, 1970

Throughout the late 1960s and '70s Toyota imported a bewildering array of family cars. All of them, from the humble Corolla to the opulent Crown, employed the tried-and-tested layout of an inline petrol engine at the front powering the rear wheels. Toyota was, then, far more concerned with proving its quality credentials than with innovation.

During a period when models were updated constantly, the medium-sized Carina family car was something of a rock, on sale from 1970 to 1977 virtually unchanged – which is why it's the Carina we've included here.

More expensive than the equivalent Morris Marina but cheaper than the market-leading 1.6-litre Cortina, the Carina was in the thick of the medium-sized family saloon sector – Britain's most hotly contested at the time. The Carina might well have sold a lot more were it not for stringent import quotas on Japanese cars.

It arrived in October 1971, and only this four-door body style was offered with a semi-fastback body. Mechanically, it was derived from the bigger Corona, with its MacPherson strut front end and a beam rear axle.

The well-equipped Carina even included an automatic electric aerial as standard, just to stick it to Western rivals.

WHO LOVED iT?

You still risked castigation, or teasing, from your friends and neighbours if you bought a Japanese car, so the Carina would have appealed to the most assertive of British consumers ... or else someone at the end of their tether with British Leyland.

There were servo-assisted front disc brakes and a choice of four-speed manual or automatic transmission with the sole 1.6-litre twin-carburettor engine on offer.

The Carina was quite a vigorous performer, able to make the 0–60mph sprint in a tidy 12.2 seconds and thrash its way up to 100mph. It was notably well-equipped and quiet, with the driving position immediately comfortable.

The Carina's fussy back-end styling concealed a good car, with surprisingly vivacious performance.

Triumph Stag, 1970

Italian design consultant Giovanni Michelotti had created the styling for every new Triumph since the 1959 Herald, and the Stag concept – a full four-seater convertible using the Triumph 2000 saloon as its basis – was actually his own idea back in 1965. The folks at Triumph liked his proposal, and decided to make it.

The padded, T-shaped roll-over bar was a unique feature. It helped strengthen the 2000-type monocoque body frame once its roof section had been chopped off. The Stag's engine choice, though, was controversial. It used Triumph's untried double overhead-camshaft 3-litre V8, essentially two Triumph 1.5-litre slant four-cylinder engines joined together on a common crankshaft.

Rover's fully sorted 3.5-litre V8, readily available to Triumph after British Leyland's formation in 1968, would have suited the car perfectly. But Harry Webster, ex-Triumph, was British Leyland's new chief engineer.

WHAT THEY SAID AT THE TIME
'The Stag is one of those cars which you appreciate the more you drive it. It has an easy and relaxing way of packing many miles into each hour, and it is a satisfying and spirited car to drive fast.' – *Autocar* magazine in July 1970 on the £2,173 Stag automatic.

The gorgeous lines of the Stag were from the pen – and imagination – of Italian stylist Giovanni Michelotti.

He was determined his cherished new power unit, on the drawing board since 1963, must have its day.

The engine became the Stag's Achilles' heel. The water pump was mounted too high (between the V of the cylinder heads), so if the coolant level dropped the pump would be left literally high and dry, and overheating became a notorious Stag fault. Blown cylinder head gaskets and poor quality control led to even more warranty claims, and so the gorgeous-looking Stag became a British Leyland liability. Ironically, many individuals did convert their Stags to trusty Rover V8 power, in which form the car worked extremely well, even though a Triumph V8 could, given fastidious care, still be perfectly reliable.

With 145bhp, performance was potent, with a claimed 118mph top speed and a 9.3-second 0–60mph time. The Stag was well behaved around corners, boasted a comfortable ride, and was a refined cruiser. And this was the first British car to feature an inertia-operated fuel cut-off in the event of an accident.

The Stag's problems were mostly resolved in the MkII of 1973. The engine was reworked, a smaller steering wheel enhanced driving

WHO LOVED IT?

As there was nothing else quite like it, the Stag had few rivals, perhaps apart from the much more costly Mercedes-Benz 350SL. Owners were prepared to put up with a few niggles but dealers struggled to cope with engine failures, and the Stag couldn't shake off its poor reputation.

responses, seating was improved, and attractive five-spoke alloy wheels were fitted. But sales failed to respond. Just 25,939 Stags had been sold by 1976, and it wasn't replaced. It was a maddening lost opportunity.

An optional hard-top option made the Stag snug for winter driving, and a match for the Mercedes-Benz 350SL.

Vauxhall Viva HC, 1970

Vauxhall made its last Viva in 1979 – which now seems an absolute lifetime ago. By then, despite the Viva's astonishing reputation for dependability, cars like the new Vauxhall Astra, with front-wheel drive and a hatchback, were the future.

The original 1963 Viva was Vauxhall's belated compact economy car to counter the Ford Anglia and Triumph Herald, and the company built a brand-new plant at Ellesmere Port in Cheshire in which to manufacture it.

Despite sharing some parts with sister General Motors company Opel, the Viva's rather severe 'razor-edge' lines and spacious four-seater interior were all-British. As was the engine, a 1057cc four-cylinder unit putting out 44bhp. Drive was to the rear wheels via a four-speed all-synchromesh gearbox, and steering was rack-and-pinion. Its replacement proved even more popular. The all-new Viva HB was longer, lower, wider and roomier, with new coil-spring suspension all round and a bigger (1159cc), gutsier

The pointed grille centre was a Viva HC trademark, as was its barrel-sided body for additional interior space.

engine; 556,752 HBs were made until 1970.

On a slightly longer wheelbase than its predecessors, the HC was roomier too, with barrel-sided bodywork giving much-needed extra elbowroom inside. In addition to 1.2- and 1.6-litre engines, Vauxhall engineers shoehorned in 70bhp 1.8-litre and 110bhp 2.3-litre lumps, too.

The car was offered in a bewildering number of derivatives: two- and four-door saloons, two-door estate and two-door coupé Vivas; Firenza coupés; and the upmarket Magnum in all three body styles but only with the larger engines. In 1971 the millionth Vauxhall Viva rolled off the Luton production line and, seconds later, the 1,000,001st example was completed at Ellesmere Port. Of HCs, there was a final roll call of 640,863.

To many, the Viva will always evoke ultra-reliable, easy-to-live-with motoring from a time when roads were emptier and driving was unhurried.

This stylish but short-lived (six months only) Firenza 2000 SL Coupé was one of many Viva HC spin-off models.

The Viva's calling card was mechanical simplicity, and many buyers liked just such a car that was easy to understand and cheap to repair. A good basic runaround with a smattering of Detroit style to it.

Alfa Romeo Alfasud, 1971

The Alfasud was everything that Alfa Romeo fans could have hoped for from the hallowed Italian company: eager, fine-handling and stylish. Yet, for once, it was aimed at family motorists on a reasonably tight budget.

The Alfasud was a joint project between state-owned Alfa Romeo and an Italian government industrial development agency, with the specific aim of bringing new jobs and prosperity to southern Italy. A spanking new factory was constructed in Naples to build it, hence 'Alfa Sud', or Alfa South. Meanwhile, Alfa Romeo in Milan oversaw the car's all-new design and engineering.

It was Alfa's first front-wheel drive car, freeing up plenty of space inside for four adults, and the engine was a flat-four-cylinder 'boxer' 1.2-litre unit positioned to sit low between the front wheels and so reduce the centre of gravity to give surefooted and fun handling.

There was slight disappointment that the Alfasud didn't possess a hatchback, despite its truncated appearance (one was finally added in 1980), but the car was such a joy to drive that owners forgave it. Still, they had to endure sometimes patchy quality. The early cars, too, came with just a four-speed gearbox, but that was rectified in spectacular fashion with the five-speed, two-door Ti model in 1974. This little car had more powerful engines, wider wheels, front and rear spoilers and four headlamps. For a short time before the arrival of the fuel-injected Volkswagen Golf GTi in 1976, it was the most exhilarating small car in the world.

A wonderful car to drive and not bad looking, either: the original Alfasud.

WHO LOVED iT?

Motoring journalists couldn't get enough of the Alfasud, loving everything about the way it drove, and were only slightly critical about the sparse, cheaply finished interior. Daring buyers who needed an economical runabout took note, although the idea of an Alfa Romeo as a daily driver didn't catch on too strongly in the UK.

This is the four-door version; there would be a long wait – nine years – for the shape to gain the hatchback it clearly called for.

WHAT THEY SAID AT THE TIME

'Although the acceleration is rather sluggish, the Alfasud upholds the sporting Alfa Romeo tradition, with its superb handling, roadholding and high cruising speed. An excellent driving position – the steering column is adjustable – and swift, light gear change are further assets.' – *Motor* magazine in September 1973 on the £1,399 Alfasud.

Datsun Bluebird, 1971

You realise, with a distance of forty years, that there must have been a concerted whispering campaign against Japanese cars in the early 1970s – including for the Datsun Bluebird.

I used to see dozens of these Bluebirds running around in the north of England when I was a kid, but was given the impression that they were rather inferior to the Ford Cortina against which they competed, and that people who bought them were misguided. Today, I think this was down to straight anti-Japanese bias.

The Bluebird may not have had the image of a Cortina but it was considerably more advanced. Even the previous-generation 1967–71 510 Series Bluebird had all-round independent suspension front and rear, and so did this new 610 range, introduced in 1971 and sold in the UK as the 1.6-litre 160B and 1.8-litre 180B. These new cars, moreover, came with a modern range of overhead-camshaft four-cylinder engines, once again upstaging the Ford.

Controls were light and the cars were softly sprung, not encouraging hard cornering, although there was a twin-carb 180B SSS offered in pillarless two-door coupé form with a five-speed gearbox (nothing equivalent came from Ford) that was quick in a straight line and could top the ton.

The Bluebird, with its independent rear suspension, was a more sophisticated design than the equivalent Ford Cortina.

What people really appreciated in the Bluebird, even in the earliest £1,240 160B saloon that first arrived in British showrooms in 1972, was the full roster of standard equipment. This included a radio, clock, reversing lights, hazard warning lights, a locking petrol cap and a heated rear window. Most of this stuff cost extra on British models at a similar price level.

WHAT THEY SAID AT THE TIME

'The four-door body is wide and has ample room for five adults, and the tinted glass keeps the interior cool and private.' – *Daily Mail* in October 1976 on the £2,380 Bluebird 180B.

Datsun was a participant in 1970s rallying to promote its image, using toughened-up Bluebirds; they did well on the East African Rally.

WHO LOVED iT?

For car buyers who did their sums, the Bluebird made an enormous amount of sense as a family car as saloon, estate (this load-carrier had leaf springs at the back, it should be added, for robustness) or coupé. The Bluebird was starting to shape motorists' expectations in suburban Britain.

Fiat 127, 1971

Here's another once-ubiquitous Fiat that would be an extremely uncommon sight on any road today. Rust and failed MOTs packed almost all of them off to the scrapyard long before they could join the classic car bandwagon. So it's easy to forget that the 127 really was a game-changer.

It was the founding member of what became known as the 'super-mini' class. It featured a transversely mounted engine at the front, driving the front wheels – just like the influential Mini itself – but then had a larger, more comfortable passenger compartment within a still-compact 'two-box' profile (one box for the engine, another for the car's body).

Fiat's 127, however, lost out to the Renault 5 in being the first hatchback supermini, for initially it was a two-door product only. Fiat hastily added a tailgate third door in 1972 to counter Renault's deft move, and so at least was the second out of the traps. Nonetheless, the afterthought hatch sill was too high, meaning a hernia-inducing heave to get heavy luggage over its threshold.

WHAT THEY SAID AT THE TIME

'At high cornering forces on dry roads, the 127 feels very safe; the rear end can develop a very slight wander under these conditions, perhaps as the rear wheel comes off the ground.' – *Motor* magazine in October 1971 on the £799 Fiat 127.

The 127 was an extremely neat little car, and a deserved massive seller for Fiat.

There were already millions of drivers who adored the Mini but were sick of its limited space and uncomfortable driving position. For them and other family motorists seeking a thrifty four-seater, the 127 was a blessing.

Once Fiat hurriedly added a hatchback to its 127 it became a bona fide 'supermini'.

There was much in common with the 128, although on a reduced wheelbase and with the 903cc four-cylinder engine from the redundant, rear-engined Fiat 850.

Drivers found plenty to like in the car, which was a sparkling performer despite its 47bhp engine and four-speed gearbox, with handling that was both fun and safe at the same time. With a couple of facelifts along the way, and an engine upgrade to 1049cc in 1977, the 127 lasted until 1983 and the arrival of the even more globally popular Fiat Uno.

Land Rover Series III, 1971

The traditional Land Rover has always stood apart from the fads and fashions of other cars. Actually, it's not really a car at all but a working vehicle built on a stout separate chassis like a lorry, and with industrial-strength four-wheel drive for getting you across desert or over bog, rather than poncing around as a lifestyle accessory.

Still, since 1954 a factory-built station wagon had been part of the line-up, and rural workers and landowners often relied on the all-purpose Land Rover as family transport as much as stump-puller and cattle trailer hauler.

The short-wheelbase Land Rover station wagon – perhaps not the ideal choice for a long motorway trip.

WHO LOVED iT?

During most of the 1970s, the Series III's reign as the only fully adaptable four-wheel drive vehicle on offer continued unchallenged. But Toyota's Land Cruiser and its 4x4 Hi-Lux pick-up would gradually start to erode its dominance.

The Series III was a minor update of the Series IIA, with nothing fundamentally changed. The choice of petrol and diesel engines was unaltered (the most recent addition being a petrol straight-six introduced in 1966), but now all Landies were less intimidating to drive for the novice thanks to a gearbox with synchromesh on all four gears. There were also better, more powerful brakes, so stopping the thing was considerably less hair-raising.

Inside, a new facia was a vast improvement but on the exterior, revised surrounds for the radiator grille and the headlights made from plastic were a target for scorn from some, who felt that the all-metal Land Rover was somehow being cheapened. These changes would be the last of any consequence for another twelve years, however, when the chronically uncomfortable on-road ride would finally be tackled when the coil-spring suspension of the Range Rover usurped the bombproof, if unyielding, Land Rover leaf springs.

If you needed four-wheel drive for your country estate, then there was little else than a Landie, this one being the long-wheelbase station wagon with safari roof.

LAND-ROVER

C109 JOA

Morris Marina, 1971

The humble Morris Marina has long been an object of derision among car aficionados. Indeed, it was planned to be boringly conventional from the very start. This was the first all-new car created wholly by British Leyland, and it had one critical function: to lure customers away from Ford. There was only one way to do that and that was to copy Ford's winning formula. Fords tended to be rear-drive, reliable, boxy, roomy, vaguely American in their styling, and – most of all – simple.

In these areas the Marina was spot on, but where it came a cropper was in the technological corner-cutting British Leyland imposed. The ex-Triumph rear axle served it well but the Marina's front suspension was a lever-arm mechanism derived from the old Morris Minor, to save money. Its limitations saddled some early examples, powered by the heavy 1.8-litre engine from the

A Morris Marina 1.8 TC four-door, quite rapid but with sometimes alarming handling.

MGB, with bad understeer and disconcerting road behaviour in sudden manoeuvres on the move. Smaller-engined models, using the faithful 1.3-litre A Series engine found in many a British Leyland product, were reasonably lively, but there were only ever four-speed gearboxes, also reused Triumph bits.

Nevertheless, once the suspension was revised and the production line workers weren't on strike, it wasn't such a bad car; despite its noisiness and indifferent road manners, it worked okay, with the 1.3 estate that joined the four-door saloon and two-door so-called coupé in 1972 probably the best version. Moreover,

it proved a brisk seller, finishing in 1973 second only to the mighty Cortina in the annual sales chart. A million Marinas were built by 1978, by which time it was on its second revamp and boasted British Leyland's new O Series 1.7-litre engine. So for a cheap rush job, the Marina turned out pretty well.

WHAT THEY SAID AT THE TIME

'Bear in mind that cost-consciousness is really the key to the range. The price of the Marina saloon is the same or less than most of its rivals, nearly all of which are significantly smaller.' – *Motor* magazine in May 1971 on the £1,003 Marina 1.3 four-door Super.

Marinas on the production line at Cowley, Oxfordshire, where over 1 million were nailed together.

Ford Granada MkI, 1972

This good-looking and powerful large saloon and estate range had an important role to fulfil for Ford in Europe: its task was to replace the Zephyr/Zodiac MkIV in Britain and the Taunus 20M/26M in Germany. These were two big cars, entirely unrelated in design, that were a pair of also-rans in their respective home markets, losing sales to marques like Rover, Triumph, Opel and Mercedes-Benz due to their mediocre performance and unappealing images.

The new cars certainly rang the changes. The Consul (with a smaller engine) and the Granada (V6 only) offered a totally new structure with all-round independent suspension featuring coil springs and wishbones at the front, plus the slightly surprising reversion to front disc brakes only from the Zephyr's all-disc set-up. The styling, meanwhile, was a skilful blend of chunky, US-inspired lines with European finesse, and the opulently trimmed Granada range-topper became the first European Ford to carry the insignia of the Italian Ghia design house as a trim level.

The handsome and powerful Granada, here in GXL form, was adored by get-ahead executives.

The delineation between Consul and Granada was scrapped in 1975, when all the cars, including the truly capacious estates, became Granadas. At the same time, Ford took the opportunity to dump the unlovely V4 2-litre engine and replace it with the newer Pinto unit.

The Granada was built in both the UK and Germany, but the latter was the sole source of the desirable coupé version. This came in two styles, pre- and post-1975, but only the latter was sold in the UK, and even then only in Ghia livery.

The Granada was the first European car to come in super-duper Ghia livery, which included a fashionable vinyl-covered roof.

WHO LOVED iT?

Executive drivers stepping up from a Cortina just loved these cars, and so did anyone who couldn't quite run to a Jag. Their image was no doubt helped by the Consul's regular, tyre-squealing appearance on ITV's *The Sweeney*.

Honda Civic, 1972

This original Honda Civic of 1972 really was a great little car. It offered a well-resolved front-wheel drive package, lightness of controls and great refinement, front and rear independent suspension, a comfortable cockpit and excellent build quality.

The Civic was absolutely the right car for the era, too, as the world plunged headlong into a prolonged fuel crisis. The car came with a notably smooth 1.2-litre four-cylinder engine that made 40mpg an everyday reality. In 1973 Britain received supplies of the latest Civic with a hatchback, so it could square up to European supermini rivals from Renault and Fiat. A five-speed gearbox, automatic transmission, 1.5-litre engine and a five-door option followed soon after.

The Civic proved a breakthrough car for Honda in the USA, where it was ahead of the curve on

WHAT THEY SAID AT THE TIME

'The engine is exceptionally smooth and quiet, and endows the light, compact body with quite outstanding performance and economy. The maximum speed is nearly 90mph, for example.' – *Motor* magazine in July 1973 on the £999 Civic.

Civics came as three- or five-door hatchbacks, albeit cars with quite a high boot sill.

Honda's excellent Civic was the perfect car-about-town for the fuel crisis-torn mid-1970s.

clean-engine technology. The company developed an alternative engine for the car, the CVCC (Compound Vortex Controlled Combustion), so it easily met stringent new emissions rules enshrined in the 1973 Clean Air Act in North America while still retaining good old-fashioned carburettors. The CVCC engine head design featured an extra valve that fed the sparkplug a rich air/fuel mixture and the rest of the cylinder a lean mixture. It meant a catalytic converter was no longer needed and it could run on leaded or unleaded petrol. This power unit, though, was never sold in Europe.

The first Civic marked a sea change for Honda, as it was the company's first mass-market car with a water-cooled engine. Founder Soichiro Honda was unhappy with the change, however, leading to a rift with colleagues. They were proved right when the appealing Civic alone made the USA Honda's biggest market.

The Civic, despite its class-leading design, was something of a granny-mobile at first – probably because it was tipped towards comfort and refinement, and not outright performance.

Keeping your Car Going in the 1970s

If there is a defining trend in the British roadscape right now, in the second decade of the twenty-first century, then it's the dwindling number of petrol stations. These days, petrol retailing is a loss-leader for supermarket chains or a profitable convenience offering on motorways where high-priced juice is sold to ill-disciplined drivers who forgot to call into their local Asda. In 2011 there were only 9,000 petrol forecourts left in the UK, one in five of them operated by supermarkets.

It's all quite a contrast to the situation in 1970, when there were 37,500 petrol forecourts littering the country. About 10,000 of these were independently owned outlets, although almost all were selling one brand exclusively. The major oil companies, though, had already built large networks of petrol forecourts, and the result by the early 1970s was a significant change in the layout of the typical site.

A row of pumps with distinctive glass globes in the open air outside a workshop or car showroom was increasingly a scene from the past. The new corporate forecourts were wide, clear expanses of concrete, with a canopy roof over the pumps held aloft by a minimal

➤ This busy BP filling station, in 1972, was typical of the new style of punter-friendly, self-service forecourt that would come to predominate. The shop's groaning with merchandise, although 'food' would be restricted to Marathon and Aztec bars; note the big push on Green Shield Stamps. (National Motor Museum)

▲ Petrol station shops in the 1970s were still emporia for motor accessories and spare parts, rather than ready meals, charcoal and ice cream.

▲ The focus on tyres was moving away from remoulds and cross-plies, with the more frequently seen alloy wheels being 'shod' with radials at the burgeoning empire of Kwik-Fit outlets.

◄ This charming lady, today surely someone's grandma, is persuading 1970s drivers to stock up on motor oil, a substance most used cars got through with gusto.

number of support columns. Even then, most still had an attendant operating outside from a booth, but the overwhelming trend was towards self-service. The first self-service station had opened in 1961 in London, and ten years later they were widespread, now that reliable monitoring systems had been perfected.

These sites had the space for a shop or an automatic car wash, and both of these fixtures began

▲ Motorists valued the mechanical simplicity of cars like the Ford Escort MkII as they could save money on car servicing by working on them themselves in an era of rampant inflation.

▲ The 1970s was a period when every man worth his salt had a garage full of tools and gadgets, such as this foot pump, so that he could do routine maintenance himself.

◄ Ask yourself: do you change your oil as often as you should? These days, oil leaks are something to consider only when cars get really decrepit. Back then, you'd be getting that funnel and drip tray out every six months if you knew what was good for you.

popping up more and more as the decade progressed. Yet we were still a long way off these shops selling a variety of food beyond chocolate and soft drinks. Motor accessories and maps were the norm, with 1-gallon or 1-pint tins of oil sold either from inside the shop or from a rack on the forecourt. But cheapjack 'remould' tyres had all but vanished from the merchandise range.

Buying tyres was a changing business. Local depots faced a new challenge from the Kwik-Fit chain, established in 1971 in Edinburgh by Tom Farmer and soon found nationwide. This was the period of wholesale crossover from the old cross-ply tyres – with their structure dependent on criss-crossed layers of nylon – to the superior radials with their strong, integral steel belts. A combination of the two on the same car would make it a scary handler on damp road surfaces, leading to

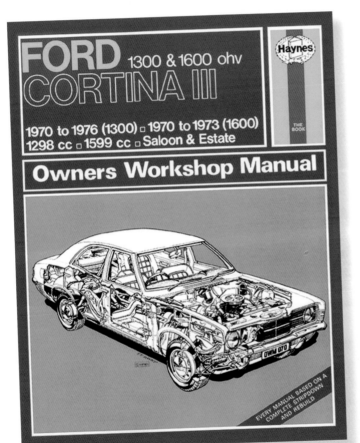

FORD 1300 & 1600 ohv
CORTINA III
1970 to 1976 (1300) □ 1970 to 1973 (1600)
1298 cc □ 1599 cc □ Saloon & Estate

Owners Workshop Manual

Haynes
THE BOOK

EVERY MANUAL BASED ON A COMPLETE STRIPDOWN AND REBUILD

◄ The average car was still simple enough to work on at home, with the carefully crafted clarity offered by Haynes Manuals helping to boost DIY confidence.

a national advertising campaign highlighting this potentially lethal combo.

Introduced in the late 1960s, the official British Standards system of star ratings for petrol octane levels was well established in the 1970s, and put an end to the sometimes confusing branding that petrol brands had used before. The pecking order went 2-star for 92 octane, 3-star for 95, 4-star for 98 and 5-star for 101.

Two-star suited low-tune/compression engines in older cars, but 3-star was fine for most modern family car engines (even though people often mistakenly fuelled them with the more costly 4-star). Powerful, high-compression engines suited 4-star, while 5-star was only needed in super high-performance engines like Jaguar's V12. Use the wrong star/octane and the engine would eventually make a 'pinking' sound that was a sign that its valves would soon be sticking to their seats, with expensive repair bill consequences. Modern filling stations offered them all through individual pumps; older and smaller forecourts usually dispensed them through multi-product dispenser pumps that would mostly vanish by 1980.

Yet the lead used to enrich petrol was being proven as extremely harmful to human beings, so lead-rich 5-star was axed in the mid-1970s. Anyway, most new cars built after 1975 could run on the unleaded petrol that would eventually dominate. Diesel fuel for cars, by the way, was still unusual, as very few diesels were manufactured and bought, and the diesel pump at the garage – if there was one – was still labelled DERV, standing for Diesel-Engined Road Vehicle!

As for prices, petrol rode the inflation rollercoaster of the era. The average gallon cost 5 shillings in 1970, which after decimalisation in 1971 became 35 new pence. At that time, about 66 per cent of

the price was taken in tax by the Treasury. By 1974 the at-pump cost was 50p, 70p in 1976 and by 1979 it was 98.25p per gallon, with the tax then at about 47 per cent. Litreage only started to be quoted alongside gallons in late 1979. The credit card was still a minority payment method throughout the 1970s, although millions of motorists redeemed Green Shield or Pink discount savings stamps at petrol stations to claw back a little of their hard-earned dosh.

So, as you can imagine, petrol, its cost and its availability, was a pressing issue for 1970s drivers. Looking after their cars was another. No car came with more than a one-year warranty, and after that DIY was the order of the day – still entirely practical as under-bonnet electronics were almost non-existent and fuel-injection was only for expensive, sporty cars. So the 1970s was the era during which Halfords prospered. Its rapid expansion, triggered by its first large branch opened in Bradford in 1973, began to put many small local car accessory shops out of business; large out-of-town motoring superstores

had to wait until 1984. Meanwhile, a publishing phenomenon that had begun in Yeovil in the early 1960s, the Haynes Manual, saw massive popularity. Unlike the factory-issued workshop manual, it showed step-by-step instructions that a car-maintenance layman could comprehend and carry out, not just a highly trained mechanic.

If your car did conk out, then there was always the AA's new Relay scheme. Introduced in 1973 for its 5 million members, it guaranteed to transport any seriously broken-down vehicle – plus driver, passengers, luggage and even trailer or caravan – to anywhere in Britain. Another innovation from the AA that year was its AA Roadwatch traffic monitoring service, going live at the same time that commercial radio launched in Britain. The AA had introduced solo motorbike scouts in 1972, to monitor road conditions in the teeth of growing traffic volumes, and their feedback proved invaluable.

But assuming you could get to where you wanted with the petrol you needed, the car in one piece and

HALFORDS MOTORING TIPS — EMERGENCY BREAKDOWN KIT

A TYRE RE-INFLATOR

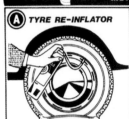

A SIMPLE PUNCTURE CAN BE EASILY TEMPORARILY SEALED WITHOUT RESORTING TO CHANGING THE WHEEL AT THE ROADSIDE. ALWAYS HAVE IT REPAIRED LATER

B TEMPORARY WINDSCREEN

YOU MAY NOT BE ABLE TO GET A BROKEN WINDSCREEN REPLACED QUICKLY – SO ALWAYS CARRY A TEMPORARY WINDSCREEN

USE GLOVES OR A DUSTER OVER YOUR HAND WHEN REMOVING BROKEN GLASS

USE ADHESIVE TAPE TO SECURE THE TEMPORARY WINDSCREEN'S EDGES

C FAN BELT

ADJUSTING NUTS AND BOLTS

WITH A BROKEN FAN BELT YOU WONT GET VERY FAR, SO ALWAYS CARRY A SPARE
– THEY ARE SIMPLE TO FIT

HALFORDS MOTORING TIPS — WORKSHOP TOOLS

A COMBINATION SPANNERS

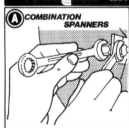

COMBINATION-RING AND OPEN-ENDED SPANNERS ARE THE MOST VERSATILE, AND CAN BE BOUGHT, EITHER SEPARATELY OR IN SETS

B SOCKET SET

SOCKET SETS HAVE A MULTITUDE OF USES, BUT WHEN BUYING REMEMBER, IT PAYS TO BUY QUALITY TOOLS – THEY LAST. AND DONT FORGET TO FIND OUT IF YOUR CAR IS A/F OR METRIC

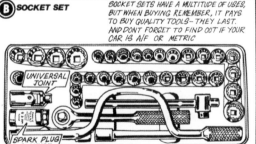

UNIVERSAL JOINT

SPARK PLUG SPANNER

C TORQUE WRENCH

IT IS IMPORTANT FOR TORQUE SETTINGS ON SOME BOLTS TO BE EXACTLY RIGHT – ESPECIALLY ON ALLOY ENGINES. ANY SERIOUS DIY MECHANIC WOULD NOT BE WITHOUT A PROPER TORQUE WRENCH

Motoring chain Halfords turned itself into a major convenience store group in this era, its huge range and competitive prices killing off many backstreet car accessory shops. Here are just some of its products.

the traffic safely negotiated, what about refreshment? In 1970 the country's motorway network boasted fifteen service areas, including such notorious sites as Watford Gap, Knutsford, Scratchwood and Toddington. In the ten years ahead the total more than trebled. The standard of self-service fare on offer, however, started to become a national joke, with Blue Boar, Granada and Welcome Break reviled, and Esso in and out of the business in three short years before its image was contaminated!

On A roads, most large towns still boasted their old-established roadhouse hotels, many of them pretty expensive and now owned by Forte, although motels – apart from the fictional one in ATV's *Crossroads*

▶ The AA's new Relay service offered to transport travellers and their stricken vehicle to their destinations, anywhere in Britain.

– were pretty rare. There were independent cafes, restaurants and truck stops everywhere in this era, when planning restraints were still light, but many drivers put their trust in the familiar red-and-white livery of Little Chef. In 1970 it had forty-four sites around the country serving brekkie all day and uncomplicated fried nosh that kids liked. By 1972 this had expanded to 100 as the company took over dozens of successful transport cafes, and there was a hungry new rival on the scene in the vivid shape of Happy Eater. There were 171 Little Chefs by 1980 and 21 Happy Eaters, but the era of a decent cappuccino that could be enjoyed on the move thanks to your dashboard cup holder was still a long, long way ahead …

◄ With 5 million members, the AA was a growing organisation in the 1970s, with ever more motorists to keep on the move.

Renault 5, 1972

Renault is the world pioneer in family hatchbacks. It produced one of the very first in the Renault 4 in 1961, and then its 1965 16 was the first five-door, five-seater hatch whose rear seat folded flat.

Now it's 1972 and France's biggest carmaker took a fresh new look at small cars, coming up with the mother of all superminis. The Renault 5 was the biggest leap forward in small car design since the original Mini. Its crisp lines embraced an airy cabin with a proper hatchback tailgate and folding back seat, turning it into a useful load-lugger.

Rivals scrambled to mimic the 5 yet its hatchback, unlike the Fiat 127 and Honda Civic, extended right down to bumper level, and there was unparalleled all-round visibility.

The car's independent torsion bar suspension gave it excellent bump absorption, even if it was apt to roll

Surefooted handling, interior versatility and a surfeit of plastic characterised the Renault 5.

Renault managed to achieve true classless appeal in the 5, just as the original Mini had, and it proved very attractive to economy-minded drivers across the board. With 5,471,701 examples sold up to 1984, the MkI 5 remains the ninth bestselling single car design ever.

The 5's chic styling was very much at home on the streets of Paris, and would become pretty familiar in London, too.

around in corners. Engine choice at first was strictly in the economy bracket, with four-cylinder 845cc and 856cc options rowed along with a four-speed gearbox.

The gear change was one of the car's few idiosyncratic features, as the gearlever sprouted from the car's plastic, one-piece moulded dashboard. There was more plastic at front and back, as the 5 was the first car with moulded glass-fibre bumpers, in light grey.

In 1979, Renault broke new ground once more by offering a five-door option in the same wheelbase and length – something widely copied during the 1980s. Sadly, though, its brilliant designer Michel Boué died in 1971 aged 35, before his clever baby was even launched.

Triumph Dolomite, 1972

This quality saloon car was a bright spot for the beleaguered British Leyland in the 1970s, presenting itself as an upmarket alternative to Fords and Vauxhalls, and even offering some credible competition to well-made German saloons from BMW and Audi.

In a tangled genesis, the Dolomite's roots were to be found in the Triumph 1300, a front-wheel-drive saloon launched in 1965 that had proved expensive to make and not especially popular. To boost sales, Triumph enlarged the engine and body to transform it into the 1500, and then expanded its range with two extra models that used a modified version of the 1500's Italian-styled body. They both relied on cheap and simple rear-wheel drive, the smaller Toledo replacing the old Herald and the larger, more powerful Dolomite aimed at former buyers of the sporty Vitesse.

At the heart of this handsome, 100mph four-door was a slant-four, overhead camshaft 1.85-litre engine, very closely related to the motor that

WHAT THEY SAID AT THE TIME

'There's no other British car quite like it, the combination of performance, luxury, refinement and driver appeal calling to mind some of the (more expensive) wares of BMW, Alfa Romeo, Fiat and indeed Saab.' – *Motor* magazine in January 1972 on the £1,399 Dolomite.

With its eager performance and quality interior fitments, the Dolomite was a refined junior executive saloon.

A Dolomite performing with the White Helmets Motor Cycle Display Team at the 1972 Royal Tournament.

The standard Dolomite found a ready place on Britain's more select suburban driveways, while the Sprint was loved by well-paid executives with a lot of driving to do. The Toledo and 1500 were both rebranded as Dolomites in 1976, such was the pull of the model name.

Triumph had long been supplying to Saab. Its responsive 91bhp could be exploited through a four-speed-plus-overdrive manual gearbox, or else savoured in a leisurely way via automatic transmission. The Dolomite was a good looker with its four headlamps and black panel behind the rear windows, while the elegant interior boasted a wooden facia, full carpeting, heated rear window, cigar (not cigarette!) lighter and a clock.

A high-performance model was to follow in 1973. The Dolomite Sprint had a showpiece engine, enlarged to 2-litre capacity and incorporating a 16-valve head – a world first in mass-produced cars – that helped its respiration produce 127bhp. The package included a Triumph TR6-spec four-speed-plus-overdrive gearbox, real alloy wheels (the first British car so equipped as standard) and not the usual go-faster fakes of the time, lowered suspension, a black vinyl roof, twin exhaust tailpipes and a purposeful chin spoiler. The performance was fantastic, with 0–60mph acceleration taking just 8.4 seconds and a top speed of 119mph. Amazing value, too, at £1,740 – a grand less than a BMW 2002 Tii.

Austin Allegro, 1973

The Austin Allegro has become something of a collector's item. True, it'll probably still be a while before one stars at a Bonhams auction, but people who love them – and there's a thriving owners' club – swear by them. It's a far cry from the mid-1970s, when the world seemed to be swearing *at* them. When new, the Allegro was unloved.

It did have a very tough act to follow: the Austin/Morris 1100 and 1300 – for most of the 1960s, Britain's bestselling motor cars. And to be fair, British Leyland tried hard to come up with an advanced replacement. The Allegro featured innovative Hydragas suspension, and went for a rounded look when the 1100 had been almost brutally straight-laced.

The thing was, the designer Harris Mann's sleek styling proposal somehow went askew in the transition from drawings to three-dimensional metal, and the Allegro turned out dumpy and unappealing. Its profile suggested a hatchback, but there wasn't one. And the car's 'quartic' steering wheel was a ridiculous gimmick replaced after just two years with a normal circular one. Where the spacious, rubber-cushioned 1100 had pin-sharp handling, the more cramped, gas-sprung Allegro could be alarmingly bouncy.

In truth, it wasn't a bad car to drive at all, and the largest engine with its twin carbs could haul it up

The Allegro aimed to shake up the family car market; most of its apparently notorious shortcomings were tabloid sensationalism around British Leyland.

'A good performer, yes, but disappointingly, not one we particularly enjoyed driving. The gear change of our road test car was very poor and the handling marred by an unbelievable steering wheel.' – *Motor* magazine in May 1973 on the £1,366 Allegro 1750 Sport Special.

WHO LOVED iT?

Not the media, that's for sure. Much of the complaints levelled at the Allegro were tabloid sensationalism, often grossly misinformed, in an era of lamentable labour relations at British Leyland. Most British buyers were happy enough with their new Allegros, with a minority unlucky enough to get a 'Friday afternoon' duffer.

to 100mph and still return 27mpg fuel economy. Engine choice was the faithful A Series as found in the Mini, in sizes from 998 to 1275cc, and a larger series of 1485 and 1748cc engines taken from the Maxi. In its twilight years, the Allegro's bugbears were mostly chased away, and it proved reliable, well-built and resilient to corrosion. No longer could it be called the 'All Aggro'. But it was all rather too late to do its reputation any favours.

The Allegro did get a stony reception from some quarters, but many of its good attributes were clear to see.

Datsun Sunny, 1973

Do not be under the impression that the Sunny was in any way a poor car. It might have been ugly, it might have seemed plasticky, and in its coupé format the headroom and rear passenger space was terrible; okay, and the ride quality wasn't especially cosseting. But what people really liked about this Datsun was its utter trustworthiness. It started on the button every morning and nothing ever fell off. All the controls were light and easy to use. And it gave a spritely enough performance for its 1171cc size (there was eventually a 1.5-litre engine option), whether in two- or four-door saloon, two-door coupé or five-door estate guise. Another enormous asset was its well-stocked specification. As one former British Leyland boss commented: 'These were cars that had a radio when even a heater was extra on an Austin; the Japanese

WHAT THEY SAID AT THE TIME

'The diaphragm spring clutch is remarkably light, while the gear change on the all-synchromesh box is excellent. The light and precise steering is by a recirculating ball system.' – *Motor* magazine in February 1974 on the £1,296 Sunny 120Y Coupé.

The dubious Americanised styling of the 120Y is easy to mock, but the owning experience was a notably trouble-free one.

These Datsuns lacked character and somehow helped to dumb down the motoring world into accepting the utterly conventional. Sensible private car buyers, spending their own money, ignored such issues, attracted by the precision engineering, excellent reliability and generous equipment. Little wonder that 5 per cent of all new cars sold in the UK in 1973 were Datsuns.

thought that was what mattered. And they were right, of course.'

What most sophisticated car fanciers would agree on was that the styling was pretty horrible, the scaling-down of redundant American car lines producing an unharmonious look, and the detail decor was tacky. Datsun in 1970 had pioneered detachable hubcaps designed to mimic alloy wheels on its 240Z, and the domed hubcaps with an intricate hexagonal pattern on later 120Ys were nothing short of hideous.

In its four-year career, the 120Y notched up 2.3 million sales – more than competitors Allegro (made for ten years), Marina (nine years) and Viva HC (nine years) combined.

The Sunny 120Y, here in two-door saloon form, almost singlehandedly turned Datsun into Britain's most dynamic Japanese importer.

The wheel trims from hell, as fitted to the 120Y Coupé, which was otherwise a decent runabout, cramped rear headroom excepted.

Reliant Robin, 1973

A chink in Britain's normally rigid licensing laws allowed Reliant's iconic three-wheeled cars to thrive for almost fifty years, despite the fact that affordable four-wheeled economy motoring was widely available for most of that time.

A 'tricycle' is classed for taxation and licensing purposes at similar rates to a motorbike, as long as its unladen weight is 500kg or less. So you can drive a Reliant on a motorcycle licence despite the fact that it has a roof, a steering wheel and no need for crash helmets. Of course, such lightness brings with it tiny fuel consumption and one less tyre to worry about, and as Reliants had had plastic bodies since 1956, rust was barely an issue either.

All of these factors made a Reliant the first choice for frugal motoring in the 1960s and early 1970s – usually the little Regal, of which the van version was the butt of many a joke on TV's *Only Fools & Horses*.

WHAT THEY SAID AT THE TIME

'All told, the Robin marks a real step forward in three-wheeler design. There is no doubt that the £10 a year tax instead of £25 is a powerful incentive to own one. Many people are also attracted by the running costs – at least 45mpg.' – *Autocar* magazine in November 1973 on the £801 Robin.

The front cover of an early Reliant Robin sales brochure, where the high-rise council estate location does little to elevate the car's aspirations.

Robin
A new idea from the ground up

The Robin's rear window was top-hinged as a sort of hatchback; the whole body was made from glass-fibre reinforced plastic.

The Robin was the most radical update of the concept so far, since Reliant hired a firm of proper product consultants, Ogle Design, to give it a neat style makeover. They brought the Reliant into line with current trends by giving it a hatchback, although this was in truth simply a rear window hinged at the top. The separate chassis, though, was virtually unchanged, still featuring Reliant's own all-aluminium, four-cylinder engine of 748cc (later enlarged to 848cc).

Just as the world plunged headlong into economic chaos and soaring petrol prices, this car could do 60mpg and be run on a shoestring. Reliant found it had an unexpected hit on its hands.

The most celebrated Reliant Robin owner was Princess Anne, who owned one as a Gatcombe Park runabout, although more typical owners tended to be from the north of England – budget-restrained manual workers who'd progressed from motorbike (single) to motorcycle-combination (married) to a Reliant (small family).

Volkswagen Passat, 1973

This spacious front-wheel-drive family car from Volkswagen took its bow in 1973 as the successor to the very popular, yet rear-engined, 'Type 3' 1600 range. Car buyers might not have twigged yet, but it was setting the template for all modern VWs henceforth, in a couple of important ways.

Firstly, of course, its front-drive packaging, with a water-cooled engine mounted at the front, was leaving all traces of the old Beetle behind. And secondly, the Passat kicked off an unapologetic cross-pollination with sister marque Audi, whose engineering was now the major influence on Volkswagen cars. In fact, VWs and Audis would never be so closely linked as this Passat and the contemporary Audi 80, as Volkswagen was happy to point out they were essentially the same car.

At the front and the back the Passat had been restyled by Italy's Giugiaro, giving it four round headlights in place of two oblong ones, and for the saloon a fastback tail treatment. At first it was simply a two- or four-door choice, but a hatchback option was added to both in 1975. There was a chunky estate, too.

The engines ranged from 1.3- to 1.6-litre and were longitudinally mounted, while the coil-sprung/trailing back axle and the front MacPherson strut suspension were pure Audi. These were all good strong cars, with excellent road manners, solid build quality and very good finish.

In case you were wondering, the word Passat is derived from the German for 'trade wind', as at the time the company was using various breezy terms for its new cars, such as the Scirocco and Golf (gulf).

WHO

LoveD iT?

Passats were always more expensive than equivalent Fords, Austins and Vauxhalls in the UK, with a well-finished but somewhat austere German feel to them. As long as you could afford them, they were markedly superior cars.

Opposite: With design assistance from Italy's Giugiaro, the Audi 80 was turned into the first Volkswagen Passat.

Passats also came in a five-door estate form, as shown here, that was an accomplished, enjoyable all-rounder.

Citroën 2CV, 1974

It does seem a trifle strange to be including a model conceived in the 1930s for hard-up French country folk, and launched in 1948, in a book dedicated to 1970s cars. Yet 1974 marked the first time since the 1950s that the 2CV had been sold in Britain, and its reappearance made quite an impact in a country where the term 'economy car' was most readily associated with the Mini.

In the 1950s, the 2CV had been assembled in Slough from French-supplied kits to get around tariff problems, but now the car was a straight export from France. And it was here in the face of economic meltdown, galloping petrol prices, and an overall reluctance from the general public to sink their money into new cars.

The 2CV was super-thrifty with its flat twin-cylinder air-cooled engine of just 602cc, and lightweight – some would say flimsy – construction, but it brought a new attitude to money-saving motoring, and that was one where slow was fun. Its top speed was a fundamentally unbearable 67mph, and getting to 60mph from rest took an epically leisurely 32.8 seconds.

The trick was to revel in the squashy seats, the absorbent ride, the bright colours, twin-cylinder racket, full-length sunroof, flip-up windows and general lack of frippery, and suddenly it was the best car in the world. Plus, it would return a very welcome 47mpg, and its willing, indomitable nature made it fantastic in the snow.

The 2CV returned to British shores in 1974; since its last time on sale here in the 1950s, the headlights had become rectangular.

WHO LOVED iT?

The 2CV started a genuine counter-culture to speediness, and won legions of ardent British admirers for its all-round cheapness, iconic design and, indeed, very practical nature. And, if you wanted a 2CV-type car with a few less draughts, there was always the similar Citroën Dyane.

The tinny little Citroën earned new respect, and generated plenty of thrills, in the 1981 James Bond film *For Your Eyes Only*, starring Roger Moore.

WHAT THEY SAID AT THE TIME

'The diminutive saloon has four doors, a roll-back sunroof, independent suspension all round, and the air-cooled twin-cylinder motor drives the front wheels. The 2CV is an attractive proposition.' – *Daily Mail* in October 1974 on the £830 2CV.

Fiat 131 Mirafiori, 1974

Every major car-making country seemed to have its own version of the Ford Cortina in the mid-1970s, and this neat saloon was Fiat's effort. Actually, it would go on to be even more successful than Ford's Cortina MkIV/80 range, with over 1.5 million examples sold, although it was in showrooms for four years more.

It was like the Cortina in that it was quite old fashioned under its neatly styled bodywork in two- or four-door saloon and five-door estate forms. The 1.3- and 1.6-litre engines were positioned inline with the gearbox mated to the engine end on, and a propshaft took the drive to the back wheels. One significant departure was the option of a five-speed gearbox.

This car replaced the old Fiat 124 and was a quantum leap forward without ever being more than utterly competent. Fiat decided to call it Mirafiori in addition to its 131 model designation, that being the name of the Turin suburb where the cars were produced.

Italy's answer to the Ford Cortina arrived in 1974 in the shape of the 131 Mirafiori; this is an early 1300CL.

The Mirafiori CL's roomy interior boasted fabric upholstery, a sculpted dashboard and Citroën-esque single-spoke steering wheel.

The whole range received an engine upgrade in 1978 when single overhead-camshaft engines replaced the old overhead-valve units at the bottom of the range, and twin-cam engines ousted the larger ones, these models being renamed Supermirafiori. A new boy racer edition was the Sport with a 2-litre twin-cam and five-speed box, quite a passable rival to the Ford Escort RS2000.

WHO LOVED iT?

The 131 was among numerous Fiats of this era that had a propensity, an enthusiasm almost, for rust. They might have been fine at home in the warm Italian sunshine, but Britain's wintry, salted road network triggered the corrosion problem immediately. This reputation always stopped the car from worrying Ford, and soon made customers wary too.

Ford Capri MkII, 1974

The Capri II presented a masterful reworking of a still-attractive basic concept. It was slightly longer and wider than the wildly popular original. The distinctive side window line with its curvaceous rear quarter window was retained even though the hockey-stick-shaped indent line and dummy air intakes on the body sides were ditched. The whole style of the car was artfully softened, modernised and cleaned up.

The most significant development was a huge hatchback-style tailgate, together with individually folding rear seat backs that, together, transformed the car's previously mediocre versatility. It was now almost a sporting estate car, like the Reliant Scimitar, although the tailgate didn't open down to bumper level, so getting heavy stuff over the threshold was hard work.

Immediately obvious was the smaller steering wheel that gave a more civilised driving position, while the MkI dashboard was otherwise carried over unchanged.

At the bottom of the Capri pile was the 1300L that retained the trusty yet mild 1298cc Kent overhead-valve motor; then came the 1600L, 1600XL and 1600GT using the 1593cc Pinto unit, and also the 2000GT with a 1993cc Pinto engine. At the top of the range was the 116mph 3000GT with the 2994cc Essex V6 under its

Many of the tacky design touches of the original Capri were erased for the smooth and modern MkII in 1974.

The big news for Capri II was the huge rear tailgate and folding seats, making the car versatile as well as sporty.

'With better sound insulation and other subtle improvements, the new car is generally more refined than the old one – and a lot more versatile.' – *Motor* magazine in February 1974 on the £1,482 Capri II 1600XL.

swoopy-looking bonnet. Most cars could be ordered with Ford's own C3 automatic gearbox and power-assisted steering. Within weeks, the top-of-the-range Capri Ghia joined them as a 2- or 3-litre.

It might have been getting creaky, especially in the face of competition from the Volkswagen Scirocco and Porsche 924, but the constantly updated Capri continued to find tens of thousands of keen new owners every year throughout the remainder of the '70s.

The Capri was at the height of its seductive powers in the mid-1970s: traditional sports cars were fading and the 'hot hatchback' revolution with fuel injection, turbochargers and five-speed gearboxes had yet to begin, so it could bask in widespread approval from enthusiasts.

Lada 1200, 1974

Transport yourself back to 1974 and you'll find yourself in the thick of a worldwide energy crisis; strikes and power cuts abound, and – in car showrooms – once-popular British marques are rapidly losing out to reliable Japanese opposition.

Once its own 124 had been discontinued, Fiat allowed Russia to export their version to the UK as the Lada 1200.

Into this chaos marches Russia's Lada. After months of market research and evaluation to gauge British reactions, the no-frills 1200cc saloon and estate went on sale in May for the first time, and by the end of 1974, 2,364 of them had found buyers.

In one way, at least, the car was already familiar to us Brits. It was the spitting image of the lately obsolete Fiat 124, and that was because the Lada 1200 was indeed a licence-built edition of the Italian family saloon.

Fiat helped the Russian state establish the Volzhsky Motor Works, 600 miles south-east of Moscow, in 1966, and it knocked out its first finished car four years later. The town supporting this vast plant was named Togliatti … after the late leader of the Italian Communist Party, Palmiro Togliatti, who brokered the 'enterprise'. But the Russian vehicles were only allowed to be exported to the West once Fiat had replaced its 124 with the all-new 131.

WHAT THEY SAID AT THE TIME

'The Lada 1200 is a thoroughly sound car, let down perhaps by the sticky steering and dead brakes. At a time when motoring costs seem to be going through the roof, this is a car which merits serious consideration.' – *Autocar* magazine in January 1975 on the £1,044 1200.

Below the familiar surface, the car had been re-engineered with a reinforced body, thicker steel panels to withstand Russia's gruelling roads and weather, and a 1200cc engine derived from a Moskvich unit. It had a heavy-duty carburettor and even a starting handle so that a flat battery would be no impediment to a freezing Siberian start. The Fiat's rear discs were replaced by drum brakes. A 1.5-litre version was added in 1977, and any lack of refinement in either was compensated for by their utter toughness.

Britain's motor trade might have mocked the vehicle, but by 1979 nearly 70,000 Ladas had been sold here and the Russian make took 1 per cent of the total car market. And the 1200 would be around for another three years before being replaced by the Riva.

WHO LOVED iT?

The reason these Ladas were so popular from the off was simple: they were so competitively priced (or, should we say, artificially low-priced because of Russian 'dumping') that they made some used cars look expensive.

In 1974 you could have this capacious Lada 1200 estate for just £1,078, against a cramped Mini Clubman estate for £1,254. Whatever their shortcomings, Lada sales exploded.

1970s Dream Machines

In 1970, the brand-new yet entirely useable four-seater supercar everyone was marvelling at was the Citroën SM. In 1980 the same excitement and longing was bestowed on the Audi Quattro. They make for a fascinating comparison.

The SM was a technical masterpiece, its 2.7-litre Maserati V6 engine driving the front wheels, while its hydropneumatic suspension, self-centring steering and powered brakes made it a unique driving experience. Space-age inside and out, the headlights turned with the steering. The Quattro, meanwhile, was also a sensational car to drive, but for entirely different reasons. The car featured four-wheel drive (soon to be allied to anti-lock brakes) and a turbocharged 2.2-litre engine; in fact, it was the first time ever that 4x4 and a turbo had been combined. In looks, it was Germanic and boxy, yet unmistakeable.

The point of comparing these cars is to show how the idea of an 'ultimate' car evolved throughout the 1970s. It had begun with almost wilful technical complexity and a reliance on exotic engines for power and prestige, plus sensational styling, and ended with a no less complicated car but one where the outer design was subtle and the ferocious performance delivered with an emphasis on safety.

▼ The hugely influential Audi Quattro was the first car to offer the potent cocktail of a turbocharged engine and performance-orientated four-wheel drive.

◀ At the beginning of the 1970s the Citroën SM was the last word in automotive modernity and fascinating technology.

The rest of this book is given over to the sensible and rational cars that most of us were forced into driving in this period, and there is perhaps a perception that the 1970s were characterised by dreary machines whose notoriety derived from their unreliability rather than their romance. But this is not true. The decade saw the emergence of several supercar legends and numerous other cars that delivered motoring thrills in contrasting ways.

There has rarely been a car as instantly sensational as the Lamborghini Countach, first revealed to a near-disbelieving world in 1971 and then, joyously, released on to the road in 1974. It was a wedge-shaped dream machine freed from the motor show halls and made real. Under the amazing, wedge-like body with its scissor-type doors was a tubular spaceframe chassis with a

V12 engine mid-mounted and the gearbox between the two seats. It could manage a reputed 170mph.

The Countach, which went on UK sale in late 1973 at £16,314, making it the country's most expensive new car, was the supercar on every schoolboy's bedroom wall. But as you might have expected, Ferrari wasn't going to let this impudent interloper trample all over its carefully crafted image as provider of the planet's most exciting cars. Arriving in Britain at about the same time was the first small consignment of 365GT4 BBs – the iconic Berlinetta Boxer. For your £15,492 you also got 170+mph performance, but the

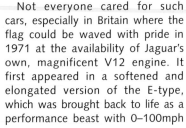

◄ The ultimate motoring pin-up of the 1970s was the Lamborghini Countach, an extreme supercar in every way, including in its scissor-type doors.

twelve-cylinder engine was mounted flat behind the driver. It was the Ferrari Daytona replacement, and as such always a little more user-friendly than the Countach.

Not everyone cared for such cars, especially in Britain where the flag could be waved with pride in 1971 at the availability of Jaguar's own, magnificent V12 engine. It first appeared in a softened and elongated version of the E-type, which was brought back to life as a performance beast with 0–100mph

◄ Not everyone was too enamoured of the styling of Jaguar's new XJS, but there was no doubting its ability as an awesome, continent-shrinking GT express. Looks pretty cool these days …

▶ The venerable E-type received a late-life fillip after Jaguar used it as a showcase in which to debut its superb 5.3-litre V12 engine. Now it was a proper 150mph road rocket.

acceleration in 15 seconds and a proper 150mph maximum speed, as opposed to the false claims of yore. As with all Jaguar power units, their main business was in propelling luxury saloons, and in this the V12 turned the fabulous XJ6 into the truly awesome XJ12 in 1972. It was another 150mph car that, as long as the build quality was right, disabused Rolls-Royce or Mercedes-Benz claims to build the world's best saloon car.

Then again, in 1975, Jaguar's super GT car, the XJ-S, proved highly controversial. Its accomplished ability to cover huge distances in hushed high speed was never in question, but its looks were not to everyone's taste with its flat, broad bonnet, oval headlights and 'flying buttresses' bracketing the boot lid.

The Jaguar V12 engine also found its way into the Panther Deville, an outrageous parody of a pre-war

▲ The Jaguar V12 engine inside the E-type Series III; once proven, the power unit would migrate to Jaguar saloons to power the XJ12, hailed at the time as the finest saloon car on the planet.

▲ The imposing Rolls-Royce Camargue of 1975 was one of the most expensive – and charismatic – cars Britain could offer and was much in demand in the Middle East.

◄ Seen here at the 1974 London Motor Show, the Panther Deville was a beautifully coach-built evocation of pre-war luxury saloons, and was powered by a Jaguar V12 engine. There was nothing else remotely like it.

Bugatti that took its bow in 1974. Along with the Jensen Interceptor convertible that year, the Rolls-Royce Camargue of '75 and the Bristol 412 of '76, it ensured that Britain still provided a fascinating biodiversity of super-expensive luxury cars with appeal to the mega-wealthy worldwide. Nowhere else could you find a parade of individualistic cars like these.

The Range Rover, meanwhile, had the upmarket off-roader scene all to itself for the whole ten years, and it was significant that its single three-door/3.5-litre V8 specification barely changed in that time, with a luxury makeover coming only in 1980, a four-door option a year later, and automatic transmission later still. Even as a second-hand car it was well beyond the pocket of most, if not to buy then to fuel and maintain.

Of expensive sports cars with their engines, racing car-style, behind the driver's shoulder, the 1970s can boast a galaxy. The mid-engined Lamborghini Urraco, Maserati Bora and Ferrari 308 GTB from Italy faced an exciting challenge from Lotus with its 1974 Esprit, a car whose appeal went global after its submarine appearance in the 1977 James Bond film *The Spy Who Loved Me*. But in many ways the rear-engined Porsche

➤ The Range Rover, seen here in its original 1970 guise, had the decade to itself when it came to sophisticated off-road motoring.

▲ This is the 365GT Berlinetta Boxer, a mid-engined replacement for the fabled Daytona. It arrived in the UK in 1974 as the ultimate modern Ferrari.

➤ Even if you rarely spotted an Esprit on the road, you would have seen it at the pictures, in the memorable 'submarine' scene from the 007 adventure *The Spy Who Loved Me*.

▲ Lotus's mid-engined Esprit might have boasted a mere 2-litre four-cylinder engine, but the two-seater was every bit as dramatic and exciting as any Italian equivalent.

911 outshone them all, for the driver who took fast motoring seriously and practised it as an exacting art, when it underwent its Turbo transformation in 1974. There was only ever a four-speed gearbox but the 153mph 911 Turbo was genuinely a racing car refocused to road use, with 260bhp on tap, a Countach-mauling 0–100mph in 14 seconds in prospect, and a 'tea tray' rear spoiler that looked, and did, the business.

Our review of 1970s fantasies would not be complete without mention of two perhaps unexpected additions to that decade's lusted-for line-up.

Just as turbocharging had brought spectacular new life to the Porsche 911, so it did again to the Saab 99 in 1977 and its later 900 derivative in '78. The excellent chassis of these cars proved more than up to the task of handling the hike from 118 to 145bhp, thanks to well-calibrated fuel injection. Acceleration was lightning quick and 120mph for these heavy cars seemed like a breeze.

The European Car of the Year for 1977 was certainly a first for a sports car. But even more surprising was the victory of Porsche with its 928. This totally new, front-engined GT with a 4.5-litre V8 engine offered fantastic handling and a 140mph top speed, exacting German build quality and a unique 2+2 shape with flip-up headlights and migraine-inducing chequered upholstery.

▲ Porsche's 1974 911 Turbo was the last word in neck-snapping acceleration, with its huge rear 'tea tray' spoiler vital to keeping it glued to the tarmac.

Volkswagen Golf, 1974

In 1972 Volkswagen built its 15,007,034th Beetle, the significance of this long-winded number being that it was one more than the Ford Model T, until that moment the bestselling single car design of all time. Yet the Beetle was already earmarked for retirement because VW was putting the finishing touches to a radical replacement: the Golf.

It was a step change for Volkswagen and also for the wider car market. Where the Beetle had been rear-engined and rear-wheel drive, the Golf's engine was at the front driving the front wheels. The Beetle's power unit was an air-cooled flat-four, but this new car had a water-cooled engine mounted transversely.

The Beetle was supplied as a two-door saloon with its unmistakeable sloping-back shape and separate mudguards. Now the Golf adopted a boxily drawn 'two-box' shape rather like the Alfasud and Citroën GS but unlike the Ford Escort and Hillman Avenger that led the small family car sector. Italy's Giorgetto Giugiaro was the consultant designer. For the Golf, there was also the practicality of a fifth door and folding rear seats.

At a stroke Volkswagen, with major input from engineers at its Audi subsidiary, had set the template that all of its rivals would follow (although it did allow the Beetle to keep rolling alongside it for many years to come). The Golf was unveiled to widespread amazement in May 1974. There were two engines, at 1073 or 1471cc, both

The shape of cars to come was defined by the outstanding new Volkswagen Golf in 1974; shown here is one of the earliest British imports.

'Lots of room inside, good handling, but a harsh ride. Good performance and economy but heavy brakes. A strong contender in its class, but expensive.' – *Autocar* magazine in February 1975 on the £1,602 Golf L three-door.

with a four-speed gearbox, three- and five-door body styles, and trim levels entitled L, S and LS.

Volkswagen cleared its gigantic Wolfsburg plant to manufacture the Golf. This was the place where the Beetle's legendary reputation for quality had been forged, but from April 1974 the Golf took its place on the production lines. As the fortunes of the place rested on the Golf's success, it was a great relief that it shot to the peak of the German new car sales charts within months. An automatic, the legendary fuel-injected GTi, the highly influential Golf diesel and the equally trendsetting Cabriolet were all to come.

In 1979 it was possible to have all the purposeful looks of the GTi without the feisty engine, in this limited edition Golf Driver.

WHO LOVED iT?

The Golf actually got off to a hesitant start in the UK. British family car buyers were so accustomed to the dated and uninspired products of domestic manufacturers, or value-packed but technologically stale imports from Japan, that they viewed this radical German interloper with caution.

BMW 3 Series, 1975

BMW created one of the very first executive sports saloons with its 1500 model of 1962, and then shrank the concept down a size for the compact

and sporting '02' series of cars from 1968 onwards. Nonetheless, the properly compact BMW saloon really came of age with the introduction of

the first 3 Series cars in 1975, and it was from this point that increasing numbers of BMWs started to be seen cutting a swathe through British

WHAT THEY SAID AT THE TIME

'From a standing start, it gets to 60mph in 10.2 seconds, the quarter mile in 17.3 seconds, and 100mph in 36.8 seconds. It does this with great and delightful zest as its predecessor did, plus a smoothness which remains a standard-setter to other makers of 2-litre four-cylinder engines.'
– *Autocar* magazine in November 1975 on the £3,446 320.

BMW's first 320 came with a four-cylinder engine, a unit praised for its uncommon refinement in this quality sports saloon.

urban traffic and tearing up our motorway miles.

Despite carrying over much of the hardware of the previous generation '02' cars, there was now a wheelbase extended by 2.5in to make the cabin less cramped, there was excellent rack-and-pinion steering, and there was a fastidiously detailed new body style – with two doors only, for the whole of this car's life in showrooms – that was sleek, discreet and tasteful.

The 320i was the initial figurehead of the E21-codenamed range in 1975 with its fuel-injected, 2-litre, four-cylinder engine. Other options were the 1.6-litre 316, the 1.8-litre 318 and a less athletic 2-litre 320 with carburettor. Both the 2-litre cars featured four round headlamps, the others just a pair.

However, the 320i was to have but a short stint in the UK price lists. In 1977 it was ousted by the 320-6, which had lost its injection and 3bhp of power but had gained two extra cylinders in its new straight-six M60 engine, which made for even more

The neat and elegant styling of the 3 Series was integral to BMW's burgeoning 1970s prosperity; it made owners appear neat and elegant, too.

silkiness in everyday driving. There was, in addition, the first 143bhp 323i. Some said this one was rather too spirited and tail-happy for its own good, and that made the new 320-6 the connoisseur's drive.

Costly though these cars were in comparison with British equivalents, they unquestionably laid the cornerstones for BMW's widespread success today.

WHO LOVED iT?

A fairly exclusive car that appealed to the well-heeled in London and the Home Counties – people who didn't mind stumping up a considerable premium for BMW's precise build quality and carefully cultivated image.

Chrysler Alpine, 1975

One of the truly forgotten cars of the decade was this reasonably handsome five-door hatchback. The Alpine presaged family cars of the future; its front-wheel drive gave surefooted handling and a spacious cabin, while the rear tailgate and folding back seats were highly practical. What's more, the Alpine was a genuine Anglo-French co-production in an era when cross-border designs were far from the norm.

Since America's Chrysler by 1966 owned both Simca in Paris and the former Rootes Group (Hillman, Humber, Sunbeam etc.) in the West Midlands, it insisted the two divisions pool their resources. Their first effort, the Chrysler 180 of 1970, was something of a lemon, but the Alpine was bang on.

The French side in Paris was responsible for the engineering, specifying Simca's dependable if noisy four-cylinder engines and four-speed transmission from the Simca 1100. Meanwhile, British stylists in Coventry carried off an excellent job with the exterior styling and spacious interior. It turned out to be such a well-executed package that it scooped the coveted European Car of the Year award in 1976.

There were differences between the two sides, though. For one thing, the French decided they were not ready to sell Chryslers, instead naming the car the Simca 1307; for the British market the sporty Alpine model name was dusted off and reused. Also, as manufacture got under way in Simca's Paris plant in

Chrysler's five-door Alpine was an interesting choice for 1976 European Car of the Year and yet widespread success seemed to elude it.

Not enough people, evidently, as deeply conservative buyers stuck with the conventional Ford Cortina; they even felt more at home with the Morris Marina. Against the mighty Cortina, too, the Chrysler took a pounding, its top-range 1442cc engine outshone by Ford's gutsier 1.6- and 2-litre motors. The issue of a separate boot was addressed by the Alpine-based Solara saloon in 1980, but by then it was too late to change the Alpine's destiny to nowhere.

1975, Chrysler UK was staving off insolvency, and the cars didn't start rolling off the Ryton production lines until mid-1976.

Most buyers should have been pleased with the car, despite its coarse and unrefined 1.3- and 1.5-litre engines, and initial lack of a five-speed gearbox. Yet it really didn't click with British buyers, and just to confuse people further, the Chrysler name was usurped by Talbot in autumn 1979 after the US company sold its ailing European arm to Peugeot. But the Alpine was still an important bridgehead between old and new technology in mass-market cars.

WHAT THEY SAID AT THE TIME

'British buyers who are used to thinking of car classes in terms of cubic capacity should modify their thinking where the Alpine is concerned, to take in available space as well. Good performance and reasonable ride, high standard of equipment and fittings.' – *Autocar* magazine in February 1976 on the £2,484 Alpine S.

The Alpine/Simca 1307 undergoes final high-speed tests at Simca's test track near Paris, just before the car was unveiled.

Citroën CX, 1975

This is the pinnacle of all the adventurous technological know-how Citroën had accumulated ever since unleashing the amazing DS on a sleepy motoring world in 1955. It offered most of the features of the sensational SM sports saloon but as a large four-door with astonishing aerodynamic lines and a sharply cut-off tail.

The SM drivetrain was manifest in the CX's unique integral self-levelling suspension, hydropneumatically linked to the four-wheel disc brake system, and its speed-adjustable power steering that was featherlight for parking manoeuvres, surefooted at high speed, and featured a self-centring mechanism. It was immediately cosseting to travel in

and, once the sensitive controls had been mastered, possessed excellent handling.

The single-spoke steering wheel was familiar from older Citroëns, but

A moody image of the Citroën CX 2400 Pallas, the most advanced large saloon car in the world at the time.

WHO LOVED iT?

This was the key car of the time for motoring technophiles, and such folk – typified by the prosperous architect – who knew the car well became its avowed disciples. The high-tech bits always worked well, if properly maintained, but problems in the routine electrical and structural parts tended to let the car down.

control stalks had been replaced by rotating drums beside the steering column, so no CX driver ever had to take one hand off the wheel.

Possibly the car's biggest letdown was in its engine department – literally. This had been designed around a compact rotary engine, but when that idea was dropped on cost and reliability grounds there was only room in there for four-cylinder units fitted transversely. Hence, the cabin always felt huge but many CXs were a little underpowered until the fuel-injected 2.5-litre GTI Turbo model came along in 1985 and could hit 137mph.

To turn the car into a limousine suitable for French politicians, the Prestige was launched with a wheelbase stretched by 8in – the same, in fact, for that in the absolutely cavernous CX estate cars. That meant the Prestige was, for its time, the roomiest standard production saloon in the world. Another CX accolade was that the 2.5 Turbo-D was, at 121mph, the fastest diesel-engined car on sale in 1983.

'There is no doubt that the ride and handling are significantly better than anything else in its class. There is more noise than one would expect and it would be a much more likeable car with lighter steering.' – *Autocar* magazine in May 1975 on the £3,262 CX 2000.

At the helm of the CX 2400 Pallas; its fingertip controls meant the driver's hands never had to leave the single-spoke steering wheel.

Ford Escort MkII, 1975

There was nothing terribly radical in the comprehensive overhaul of the top-selling Escort, which had been around largely unchanged since 1967. Even the all-new styling, while certainly tidier, was plain and simple rather than eye-catching, and all the mechanical elements were pretty much identical.

This is how engineers collected data from prototypes in an era before computers and mobile phones. Here, the Escort MkII is being readied for public sale.

The MkII, however, offered a welcome evolution, with a better ride thanks to softened suspension on most versions, better seats, and improved all-round visibility. And whereas, previously, larger engines had been strictly for the performance models, now you could have a less frenetic 1.6-litre Pinto engine in GL and all-new Ghia trim.

Even the 1.3-litre engine allowed a 0–60mph acceleration time of 13.5 seconds – lively stuff for a small car in those far-back days. But there was always the expectation that a MkII

Escort could handle much more urge, and in October 1975, nine months after launch, Ford announced the RS1800, with a specialised, Cosworth-built, twin-cam engine giving 115bhp. This RS (Rallye Sport) 1800 was built in limited numbers to qualify the Escort for rallying, and it

WHAT THEY SAID AT THE TIME

'Although the Escort Popular is no great speed machine, it is not the crude, unacceptable basic vehicle which some other countries will happily accept, but a proper motor car for which we predict a further addition to the success currently enjoyed by the Escort.' – *Autocar* magazine in July 1975 on the £1,299 Escort Popular.

proved spectacularly up to the job, clinching the Manufacturers' World Rally Championship for Ford in 1979; the RS Mexico and RS2000 – with new nose, spoilers front and rear, and alloy wheels – were the more user-friendly 'hot' MkII Escorts that saw all the benefit of this heroism. Boy racers enjoyed bronze-tinted glass and Recaro front seats.

A bit more pertinent to the average motorist was the Escort Popular of July 1975, a super-basic 1.1-litre economy edition, with all-drum brakes and cross-ply tyres, for a car market undergoing one of its worst austerity periods.

WHO LOVED iT?

The Escort MkII was on sale for just four years, with almost 650,000 examples sold. It was an updated godsend for cautious buyers who still didn't trust front-wheel drive hatchback alternatives. Plus, the nimble, lightweight Escort was both easy to drive for the timid and rewarding for the enthusiast.

Political maverick Screaming Lord Sutch, of the Monster Raving Loony Party, sensing victory in a celebrity Escort MkII support race.

In MkII form the Escort made a formidable rally machine, seen here in action on the 1976 1000 Lakes Rally in Finland.

Mercedes-Benz 200-280, 1975

'Over-engineered' is a term that might have been invented for these Mercs. They are built like rather superior tanks and they are still eminently useable – if thirsty – to run daily nowadays. First seen in 1975, the W123 was destined to be Mercedes-Benz's most successful range so far; if it was high quality, reliability and stately comfort you wanted, here it was in spades – as long as you were happy to shell out the dosh. For this was one of the most expensive 2-litre saloons you could buy; in 1976 the base 200 cost £2,000 more than the £2,928 Ford Granada 2000L, and didn't even have a radio as standard!

The range began with the sluggish (0–60mph in 15 seconds) 2-litre four-cylinder 200, and worked its way up through the 2.3-litre 230 to the

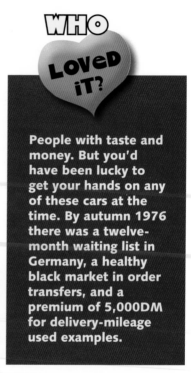

In its many varieties, the Mercedes-Benz W123 range proved enormously popular for its comfort and longevity.

six-cylinder 250 and 280 saloons offering a single-camshaft 2.5-litre and a twin-cam 2.8-litre engine respectively. The fuel-injected 280E was a 125mph express, and the W123's excellent suspension and damping was well up to the extra power. In contrast, the unbelievably rugged four- and five-cylinder diesel options were absolute tortoises. As well as the saloons, soon there were coupés, estates and even the rarity of a factory-built long-wheelbase limousine.

As mentioned, considering the steep prices demanded for all this German metal, standard W123s came sparsely equipped. You paid extra for gadgets, in-car entertainment and luxury trim. In 1970s Britain, though, this was no deterrent among Merc loyalists and these cars usually left showrooms groaning with optional equipment. By 1986 almost 2.7 million had been sold worldwide.

The 280E was the range-topper, with 125mph on offer from its fuel-injected 2.8-litre engine. Pricey, though.

WHAT THEY SAID AT THE TIME 'Excellent performer provided one revs the very willing engine. Although beautifully smooth, the engine is, as before in some Mercedes cars, clearly a slightly small one in a large body, well suppressed but still audibly a worker, except at town speeds when it is very quiet.' – *Autocar* magazine in October 1976 on the £8,066 280E.

Polski-Fiat 125P, 1975

Long before the days when Poland's best exports were its manual workers, the Communist-era country took a note out of Lada's book and decided to dip its toe into the British car market.

And just like Lada, the car it kicked off with was another obsolete Fiat. The licence agreement between the Italian giant and Poland's state-owned carmaker Fabryka Samochodów Osobowych (FSO)

was signed in 1965 and concerned the medium-sized Fiat 125. However, Fiat was anxious not to jeopardise the prospects of its own 125, so cannily specified that the engines and running gear should come from the even older Fiat 1300/1500 range. It would be a new-looking car using outdated technology, but by the standards of anything else available behind the Iron Curtain, it would be better than a Mercedes.

The Polish plant was so archaic that it took two years to prepare it for manufacturing the newly named Polski-Fiat 125P, but by the end of 1967 seventy-five examples had been built and it was soon a common sight all over the nation. An unusual bright spot of sophistication was the fitment of four-wheel disc brakes.

By the time the 1.5-litre, 75bhp car reached Britain in 1975, it was very much a creaking relic, but the rock-bottom price allayed most criticism of its basic interior, poor finish, mediocre handling and rough ride quality thanks to its old-fashioned, but tough, leaf-spring rear suspension. As it was made from poor-quality steel, rust was a bugbear, but the Poles also designed their own estate and pick-up versions. Amazingly, they would continue to be available in the UK until 1991, at which point, with a just sub-£3,000 price tag, the 1.3-litre model – by then sold as the FSO 125P 1300 – was the cheapest new car on sale.

First-class travel was not top priority with the Polski-Fiat 125P, but its economy-class cabin was at least spacious.

Always exceedingly cheap, these Polski-Fiat/FSO Cold-Warhorses provided a brand-new car, with a warranty, for the cost of a worn-out second-hand one. For many budget-conscious buyers, perhaps not living in image-conscious Hampstead or Weybridge, that was a very attractive proposition.

The Poles themselves devised this transformation into estate car form for the 125P; amazingly, you could still get one new in 1991.

Four headlights, four-wheel disc brakes, four doors and foremost in the value stakes, once you forgave the ancient engine the 125P made a lot of sense.

WHAT THEY SAID AT THE TIME

'It is keenly priced and has disc brakes all round. Laminated windscreen, tool kit, hazard-warning flashers, lighter, lockable fuel filler and reclining seats are standard equipment.' – *Daily Express* in October 1975 on the £1,349 125P.

Austin-Morris-Wolseley 18-22 Series/ Princess, 1975

This wedge-shaped saloon is yet another of those mid-1970s British Leyland efforts about which, in retrospect, it's all too easy to be contemptuous. True, it had its fair share of quality and reliability woes. But it was a forward-looking design packed with good features, and while never exactly the enthusiast's choice, it was still a good handler with excellent ride comfort.

The aim had been to make a car that rode as well as any Citroën over Britain's pot-holed road surfaces, and this it pretty much did thanks to its Hydragas suspension. Handling was pretty good, too, with front-wheel drive and the engines mounted transversely – not just the 1.8-litre four-cylinder B Series engine (signifying the '18' of the range title), but also the 2.2-litre overhead-camshaft six-cylinder E Series (the '22' bit). Both had to work quite hard in this heavy vehicle, so in performance terms the cars didn't distinguish themselves.

Where they did stand out was in their amazing styling. The roomy passenger compartment, with its

This exhibition model of a Morris 2200 HL shows the unusual transverse location of the car's six-cylinder power unit.

'Its strongest point is the astonishing amount of room inside it, coupled to a big – but rather high-silled and small-lidded – boot. The 18-gallon tank gives a safe cruising range of over 400 miles, while the styling seems to be generally accepted as strikingly attractive.' – *Autocar* magazine in April 1975 on the £2,116 Morris 1800.

110

A Princess body begins its journey through British Leyland's Cowley production process; a shame the car never really caught on.

Despite its initial impact, buyers tended to prefer cars like the Ford Consul and larger-engined Cortina, and the Princess found itself passed over by those seeking a large, relaxing family car for long-distance driving.

big squashy seats, was cloaked in a dynamic-looking fastback body with a dramatically rising waistline, deep windows, and a steeply raked windscreen and bonnet, with slants and angles everywhere. Everyone called it 'The Wedge', although some company insiders nicknamed it 'The Anteater'. A shame, then, that the hatchback the profile suggested was absent.

The car was offered in Austin, Morris and Wolseley guises, and was generally well-received until, bizarrely, after a mere six months on sale, these names were swept away and the whole range was consolidated under the newly created Princess marque. This, reeking of some sort of emergency rethink, must surely have helped towards the unloved image the car soon engendered, with initially strong sales tailing off markedly as the decade wore on.

Triumph TR7, 1975

You do need to remember the TR7 in context. It was developed in the early 1970s primarily for export to the USA, where its rattlingly crude predecessor, the TR6, seemed doomed. Carmakers genuinely believed (wrongly, as it transpired) that legislators would outlaw soft-top cars on the grounds of poor passenger protection in the event of a roll-over accident.

So Triumph management decided to make the seventh TR only as a hard-top coupé. Pop-up headlights were part of a shovel-fronted monocoque body, whose lines rose towards the rear to form a distinctive wedged profile, and spongy bumpers that rebounded into shape after a 5mph impact were incorporated to satisfy more US safety requirements. In place of the TR6's raw 150bhp power from its rowdy, smog-producing, 2.5-litre straight-six, the TR7 received a refined 2-litre four-cylinder motor giving a mild 105bhp.

It was an incredible eye-catcher at a time when the decrepit Triumph Spitfire and MGB were still prevalent. It was civilised and pleasant, with a good cabin – lurid green or red tartan upholstery notwithstanding – excellent steering, terrific handling, a great driving position and a capacious boot.

Always controversial, the Triumph TR7 was aimed at an American market where it was wrongly predicted that only new steel-topped cars would be permitted.

'Triumph's thoroughly modern TR7 may have an old-fashioned live axle but it beats its predecessors hands down when it comes to handling and roadholding … a fast and satisfying car to drive on give-and-take country roads.' – *Autocar* magazine in June 1976 on the £2,999 TR7.

This TR7, built in 1978, was used to promote Coca-Cola and pep up Triumph's image at the same time.

WHO LOVED iT?

Well, at first, the Americans lapped up the TR7. Yet despite all its modernity, it was regularly outsold by the ancient MGB. An equally big threat came from the emergence of the Volkswagen Golf GTi and the era of the 'hot hatchback', which offered potent everyday performance with superb practicality.

But open cars always feel faster than they are; without a canvas roof to throw back to let the fresh air rush in, the TR7 always seemed prosaic. Stuck inside a TR7, the driver became dolefully aware of the sedate 0–60mph time of just under 10 seconds and the 110mph top speed.

Along with a standard five-speed gearbox, the convertible did, belatedly, arrive in 1979, although the TR7 survived just two further years.

Vauxhall Cavalier, 1975

The Cavalier was a significant turn-around car for Vauxhall, reasserting the British marque in the market with quality, value and reasonable dynamism after years of churning out also-rans. It was as good as, if not better than, the Ford Cortina whose front engine/rear-drive layout

The three sporty faces of the 1975 Cavalier range that was to haul Vauxhall's image out of the doldrums.

it aped. The first Cavalier was a genuinely good car.

Sadly, its appearance signalled the end for Vauxhall as creator of its own products. With the exception of its 'droop-snoot' front end treatment, the Cavalier was designed and engineered by Opel in Germany, where a near-identical model was sold as the Ascona. Not only that, but the Cavalier was manufactured in Belgium until 1977, at which time it joined the production lines in Luton.

Once British manufacture began, there was a British engine option, too – the faithful 1.3-litre Viva powertrain in an entry-level car, in addition to the 1.6-, 1.9- and later 2-litre engines shared with Asconas. There were two- and four-door saloons and a very stylish coupé, but, surprisingly, an estate car was never offered.

The Cavalier was a car of its time, as the hard-driving, jacket-off and sunglasses-on company car driver was really getting into his stride

The Cavalier Coupé was a handsome car, and with a 2-litre engine was well up to sustained, high-speed motorway driving.

'Overall, in spite of our criticisms, we liked the Cavalier very much. It is in our opinion a tremendously good-looking car, and there is no doubt whatsoever about its good performance and very good handling, whether you are in a hurry or driving gently.' – *Autocar* magazine in March 1976 on the £2,883 Cavalier GL Coupé.

on British roads – even before the arrival of the completed M25 and cappuccinos served at Newport Pagnell Services. Early Cavaliers were thrashed to within an inch of their lives up and down the M6 by their shirt-sleeved masters, had a 'retirement' as minicabs, and then headed to a grateful death in the scrapyard. Indeed, the nameplate became a cult icon of the British roadscape, with 1.7 million Cavaliers of three distinct types sold over twenty years.

WHO LOVED iT?

The bigger-engined Cavaliers suited company car drivers, from area managers to roving reps, down to the ground. Such knights in sample armour appreciated their willing nature, tidy road manners, slick styling ... and 'fresh start' image after years of pretty unappealing new Vauxhalls.

1970s Car Culture

Of all the motoring trends to wax and wane during the 1970s, the changing fortunes of the company car were one of the most pertinent to Middle Britain. And the mid-point of the decade was also to be the pinnacle in its popularity.

Ever since the M1 opened in 1959, road access around the country evolved rapidly. Where area managers and representatives in large firms might have been confined for practical reasons to a fairly local patch, now they could travel across larger regions quickly and easily. Saloon cars of the 1960s, like the Ford Cortina, Vauxhall Victor FD, Triumph 2000 and Rover 2000, were more rigorously engineered to cope with high cruising speeds in comfort and style, and companies started to purchase them for staff who needed to do lots of travelling to meet customers or suppliers, and couldn't be expected to wear their own cars out in the process.

By the early 1970s, the company-supplied car was also well established among desk-bound managers. It

▲ An empty British motorway on an early morning in the mid-1970s … just waiting for the daily invasion of company cars and their drivers.

had become a perk as part of the job package, like Luncheon Vouchers or company sports club membership, and this expectation intensified when the government insisted on capping private sector wage rises at 5 per cent in an era when annual inflation sometimes exceeded 15 or even 20 per cent. The car made up for the lack of cash. Few large companies were thus without a fleet manager to oversee their company cars, and his needs heavily influenced several generations of popular models. When buying in bulk for aspiring

▲ The 1970s was the height of the company-car-as-free-perk period, when truckloads of Cortinas, Consuls and Granadas like this were bound for the corporate car park and ambitious, restive employees.

▲ The most influential car designer of the 1970s, Giorgetto Giugiaro, alongside the Volkswagen Golf, one of his signature shapes.

▲ Telly on the blink? Just three channels, no breakfast TV, remote control a complete indulgence, but at least rental firm Granada replaced your set if it played up, helped by company cars that served a purpose rather than just being a nice freebie for office workers. Granada bought 1,800 of these Viva de Luxe estates in 1972.

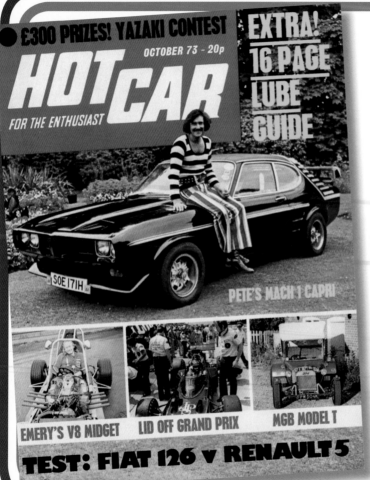

£300 PRIZES! YAZAKI CONTEST

OCTOBER 73 - 20p

HOT CAR

FOR THE ENTHUSIAST

EXTRA!
16 PAGE
LUBE
GUIDE

SOE 171H

PETE'S MACH 1 CAPRI

EMERY'S V8 MIDGET

LID OFF GRAND PRIX

MGB MODEL T

TEST: FIAT 126 v RENAULT 5

▲ Customising was all the rage in the 1970s, usually with clapped-out bangers from the '60s and '70s, but here it is carried out on behalf of Pepsi on the bestselling van/can of the time, Ford's Transit.

◄ Top-selling magazines like *Hot Car* stoked the 1970s craze for individualising your car with more power and a fancy livery, as fashion victim Pete here did in 1973 with his Mustang-engined Capri.

colleagues, he wanted a decent discount and also cars that were mechanically robust and cheap to fix, which explains the unadventurous specification of cars like the Cortina, Marina, Avenger and Viva … and the myriad engine and trim options so the cars could be closely aligned to the corporate pecking order.

Finally, in 1976 the government decided to clamp down on this 'benefit in kind', and in 1977 a scheme was introduced that taxed the company car drivers at three levels based on the engine capacity of the car: below 1.3-litre; below 1.8-litre and above 1.8-litre. The tax take would gradually increase, and the new rules acted as a spur to many new 'tax break' derivatives with engines just below 1.8-litre. It was the beginning of the end for the company car 'freebie'.

Britain officially joined the EEC on 1 January 1973, and soon there was a definite shift in tastes in car design. After years when mainstream models from firms like Ford and Vauxhall had represented American cars in miniature, the Top 10 sales charts would soon start to froth with more compact and versatile family hatchbacks as sales of the class-leading Volkswagen Golf and Ford Fiesta ramped up. The person who shaped public car taste throughout the 1970s and '80s was undoubtedly Italy's Giorgetto Giugiaro, whose skill at styling three- and five-door family cars with pleasingly clean and sharp profiles was unrivalled. In-house designers struggled to match what this gifted consultant could conjure up time after time.

It was the Giugiaro-shaped Volkswagen Golf that provided the basis for one of the real game-changers of the decade. The Golf GTi, with its powerful, fuel-injected engine, wide wheels and purposeful livery, was the first 'hot hatchback' (okay, not quite the first, as it was beaten to European showrooms by the non-injected Renault 5 Alpine by a month or two, but who remembers that car now, eh?).

Suddenly, the 'hot hatch' was the new must-have, everyday performance car – the spiritual successor to the late, lamented Mini Cooper but also outshining both sporty yet 'unsorted' coupés like the Ford Capri and the elderly crop of two-seater sports cars on offer from MG, Triumph and Fiat. None of them could hold a candle to the cocktail of the Golf GTi's handling, urgency or sheer practicality.

Not that all the fun was to be had within the parameters of German engineering and good taste. Britain in 1970 remained a nation of spanner-wielding tinkerers, with enthusiasts up and down the land building their own kit cars in their lock-up garages at home. The vogue had shifted away from plastic-bodied sports cars to beach buggies from the likes of GP and Bugle, for which there was a plentiful supply of Volkswagen Beetle MOT failures to pillage for components. Nonetheless, the component car business took a serious knee to the groin in April 1973, when VAT was introduced to bring the UK into line with the rest of Europe. Car kits, previously, had been free of purchase tax, but VAT was now levied on them. For one or two small firms, like Clan in County Durham and Ginetta in Essex, sales were decimated almost overnight, but it didn't stop other firms like

▲ Volkswagen's Golf was a significant 1970s debutante, but the sparkling GTi model was equally important, as it brought the era of the 'hot hatchback' into life, ending the elderly Mini Cooper's reign as the ultimate compact performance car.

Dutton prospering towards the end of the 1970s.

Other types of alternative car faced a rough time, too. The wedge-shaped, three-wheeled Bond Bug, with a lifting canopy instead of doors and a bright orange colour scheme, was a bit of a laugh but failed to catch on despite an all-in purchase-and-insurance package aimed at young drivers. The Enfield electric car, meanwhile, was widely trialled by electricity boards, but made little sense without incentives and subsidies – at £2,808 mid-decade, it was almost three times the cost of a Mini; it was ahead of its time but just 108 cars were built.

Customising your car became a big thing in the 1970s, the hobby spawning its own magazines and events. Usually, it was second-hand British cars given a US-style hot-rod makeover, with lowered and widened bodywork, bonnet bulges, jacked-up rear suspension with big wheels and elaborate paint jobs festooned with risqué murals or leaping flames. Ford Anglias, Zodiacs and Cortinas were favourites, while a 'sit-up-and-beg' Ford Pop from the 1950s with a Jaguar back axle was the acme. But even a standard saloon could be sexed up with wide Wolfrace alloy

▼ The actual Ford Capri Ghia, as driven by that iconic 1970s throwback Derek 'Del Boy' Trotter in BBC1's *Only Fools & Horses*, replete with tiger-skin seat covers, furry dice and a battery of extra fog lights.

wheels, go-faster stripes, long bendy aerials, a louvred rear window, furry dice dangling from the rear-view mirror and a green sunshade strip across the top of the windscreen, perhaps sporting 'KEVIN' on the driver's side and 'TRACEY' over the passenger seat. As for sounds, it was whatever could be got from analogue cassettes or eight-track stereos before the distortion became unbearable. But one noise now definitely forbidden was the ear-splitting melody emitted by musical car air horns, most commonly *Colonel Bogey*; they were banned from 1 August 1973 because they were deemed to sound too much like the new US-style sirens – the 'woo-

◄ Kit cars and beach buggies that you could build at home using a time-expired Volkswagen, such as this groovy GP, were very popular in the early '70s, but the imposition of VAT in 1973 kyboshed demand.

SOMETHING NEW UNDER THE SUN

▲ A brochure for the 1970 Bond Bug, a bright orange, wedge-shaped three-wheeler that brought some style to economy motoring, but didn't catch on. The man who styled this was also responsible for the Raleigh Chopper bike.

woo-woo' noise rather than the recognisably British 'nee-naa, nee-naa' – on ambulances and fire engines.

The four-wheel-drive phenomenon, meanwhile, was in its early days. The Range Rover was far too costly to be attainable by anyone outside the landed gentry or 'Chelsea farmers', and Land Rovers and the very few Jeeps and Toyota Land Cruisers on British roads were strictly agricultural workhorses. But there was a small stir at the 1977 Motorfair show at west London's Earl's Court, where there was a strange new Japanese car on display called a Subaru. Outwardly, a normal and fairly unremarkable small estate, underneath it had a 4x4 drivetrain. Even so, no one perceived it as an influential leisure vehicle, and most early Subaru dealers offered the cars as a sideline to their main business of tractors and farm machinery.

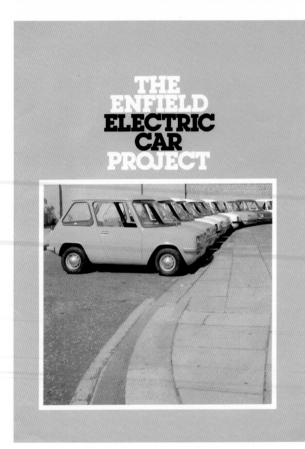

THE ENFIELD ELECTRIC CAR PROJECT

➤ Zero-emission cars are finally becoming commonplace in the twenty-first century, but the 1975 Enfield Electric was a pioneer of its type; the Electricity Council bought sixty-six of them for field trials, each costing about three times the price of a petrol-powered Mini.

Finally, it should be remembered that British car buyers began the 1970s as arch patriots and ended it in turncoat consumer treachery. By the end of 1969, imported cars accounted for just 10 per cent of the UK's total sales. However, by 1972, a quarter of all cars sold were made abroad, and by 1977 it had reached 50 per cent. By the end of 1979, 61 per cent of new cars were foreign-made, boosted by Fords, Vauxhalls and Talbots which now came from across Europe.

▼ First seen at the 1977 Motorfair, the Subaru 1600 estate looked fairly humdrum, but it was a radical new concept because it featured four-wheel drive in a normal car package.

Vauxhall Chevette, 1975

The Chevette arrived in Vauxhall showrooms in May 1975 and immediately caused a stir. This was the first British-built compact hatchback to rival the Renault 5 and VW Polo, beating the Ford Fiesta's arrival by a year and British Leyland's Metro by five.

The Chevette was the British strand of General Motors' ground-breaking 'World Car' project. The basic T-Car design was overseen by Opel, with versions of it then manufactured at GM's outposts around the world, from Chevrolet in Brazil to Holden in Australia and Isuzu in Japan. As the North American Chevrolet Chevette, it was the smallest car built in the USA. Nothing with such a global reach had ever been attempted before, although the T-Car was often heavily modified to suit local tastes and regulations. Although the hatchback was novel, mechanically the car was conservative, with old-fashioned rear-wheel drive, independent double-wishbone front suspension and a live back axle.

For the Chevette, quite a bit was unique, like the aerodynamic 'droop-snoot' front styling, imperial instrument readings in a unique dashboard, and the 1256cc engine and four-speed gearbox formerly found in the Viva. A two-speed heater fan, radial tyres, reversing lights, heated rear window and reclining front seats were standard even on the base model; the best-equipped, aside from the numerous special editions, was the 1976 GLS

Pretty much everything was right with Vauxhall's attractive Chevette in 1975, and it became Britain's bestselling small car for three consecutive years.

with velour upholstery, sports wheels, overriders, a centre console, and front door pockets.

While there was only one engine choice throughout the Chevette's nine-year life (apart from the limited-production 2300HS rally car), there were several body styles. In June 1976 there came two- and four-door saloons, while four months later a two-door estate joined them. It was always a well-balanced little car with decent rack-and-pinion steering and lively responses.

WHAT THEY SAID AT THE TIME

'It has modest performance (89mph, 0–60mph in 15 seconds) but excellent economy (we got 30.4mpg overall – careful owners get much more). The engine, through careful mounting and sound-proofing, is much quieter and smoother than that in the Viva.' – *Motor* magazine in April 1975 on the £1,593 Chevette L.

WHO LoveD iT?

For Vauxhall, the trusty little Chevette proved a huge hit, increasing overall sales by a massive 50 per cent within three months, and until 1978 it was the UK's bestselling hatchback. Brits found it the perfect compromise – good looking and practical but defiantly old-tech, so that what little there was to go wrong would actually go wrong less often.

Here is the Chevette done American style in 1976 as the Chevrolet Chevette, part of General Motors' T-Car 'World Car' project.

Ford Fiesta, 1976

Ford was a Johnny-come-lately to the supermini arena, where the benchmark car in the first half of the '70s was probably the Volkswagen Polo. But when it did finally get its act together and join the party with the Fiesta, it got everything right.

The car signalled quite a culture shift within Ford. It didn't simply repackage time-worn technology, as other Fords had done for years; it was the first really small Ford with a hatchback in the definitive supermini style as defined by the Renault 5, with the natty styling carried out in the Ford-owned Ghia studios in Italy. It was also the company's first front-wheel-drive car with a transverse engine. And it was first manufactured in Spain, in a brand-new, purpose-built plant in Valencia.

The Fiesta design began in 1973 under the codename 'Bobcat' – signifying both its short, truncated shape and one of the project's stipulations: that its production costs had to be $100 less than for the existing Escort!

Its engines weren't particularly exciting – four economical OHV units – and it came only with a four-speed gearbox, even in the early XR2

Ford barged into the supermini arena in 1976 with its front-wheel-drive Fiesta, and it was an immediate and colossal hit.

performance edition of 1981. But the Fiesta, first on sale in January 1977, immediately proved itself to be good to own and drive, at once supplanting the Chevette as Britain's favourite small car. Indeed, the car's success in Europe and globally was remarkable.

Within three years, Ford had built a million Fiestas and its $1 billion project investment had paid off handsomely. Subsequently, the Fiesta nameplate's fate within Ford has proved legendary, beaten only by the Mustang's for longevity.

A hatchback opening properly down to bumper level ensured the useful little Fiesta was one of the most house-trained superminis around.

WHO LOVED IT?

Once Ford joined the supermini sector, Britain's 1970s motorists finally felt able, en masse, to trust the genre that updated the original Mini concept so thoroughly. The MkI set in train a feat achieved by no other car: a Fiesta has been in the British Top 10 bestsellers' list without a break since 1977.

WHAT THEY SAID AT THE TIME

'This new small Ford brings a touch of flair, driver enjoyment and all-round efficiency to the small car market. It is going to prove tough competition for the cars already offered by other manufacturers. Is it worth waiting for? Yes.' – *Autocar* magazine in October 1976 on the £2,079 Fiesta L.

Honda Accord, 1976

We've become very used to Honda being one of the world's biggest and most consistently successful carmakers, but back in the mid-1970s it was something of a minnow among the pikes, still shaking off its reputation for building air-cooled oddities as the Civic started to accelerate its success. Although Honda had toyed with the notion of next introducing a sporty rival to the American Ford Mustang, it sensibly decided on a car that would be a step-up for Civic drivers or an alternative to other mainstream family cars.

To that end, the Accord, revealed in May 1976, was a neat and efficient three-door hatchback using some Civic hardware, such as its excellent coil-spring independent suspension and rack-and-pinion steering, but with a longer wheelbase. A front-drive, transverse, 1.6-litre, four-cylinder engine, a five-speed manual or two-speed semi-automatic transmission, and a general aura of mechanical refinement were all intrinsic to the car, which was pitched in size somewhere between an Escort and a Cortina.

You couldn't fail to be impressed with this smooth-running car, and Honda's excellent build quality and the low failure rate of its components meant Accord buyers were rarely at loggerheads with dealers, even if the Accord was a bit more expensive than

The superb Accord made sure that Honda hit the ground running as it took on the establishment in the family car middle ground.

The first Accord saloon of 1977, on the left, alongside an Accord of 2007 directly descended from it.

British equivalents, such as the Allegro and Avenger. But this was more than compensated for by a standard specification crammed with goodies, including cloth seats, a rev counter, intermittent wipers (rare in those days) and an FM radio. There were warning lights for doors or hatchback left ajar, and even one to tell you that a new tyre would be advisable.

WHAT THEY SAID AT THE TIME

'This is not a "standard" Japanese car with the usual depressingly compromised looks, handling, brakes and ride. We enjoyed driving it and so, we suspect, will many enthusiasts if they can overcome their instinctive prejudice. It is a challenger that everyone should take seriously.' – *Autocar* magazine in January 1977 on the £2,895 Accord three-door.

The three-door Accord's comfortable accommodation, from which the lightness of its controls and tidy road manners could be enjoyed.

WHO LOVED iT?

With a mild 68bhp on tap, the Accord had plenty of appeal to mature drivers less concerned with sprinting away from traffic lights and more with smooth driving and the Accord's commendable fuel economy; an average 30mpg was easily doable. Power steering, unusual then on sub-2-litre cars, was offered from 1978, and widely taken up.

Renault 14, 1976

Here is Renault's valiant attempt to counter the Volkswagen Golf with a well-packaged family hatchback. Beating the German icon as an excellent all-rounder was a task that the car fell short of. It simply wasn't well built enough and it had a couple of annoying design faults. Yet the 14 was extremely spacious, drove enjoyably, and looked like nothing else on the road; indeed, in early advertising, Renault compared its unusually rounded proportions with those of a pear.

And that was a mistake, too, as the car would subsequently prove to rot away, thanks to rust, almost as fast as fallen fruit.

This was the first Renault with a transversely mounted engine, which it shared with the Peugeot 104. That meant that it was mounted in a near-horizontal position, tilted over at 72 degrees, with its four-speed gearbox contained below inside its oil sump, like a Mini's. The compact

WHO LOVED IT?

The answer is, not quite enough people; Renault was hard pushed to convince punters that this car had the right qualities to lure them away from more established models, much less that it was equal to a Golf or the later Ford Escort MkIII.

Renault's stab at glory in the Golf class came in 1976 with the 14, a bold design plagued with a few annoying problems.

dimensions of this set-up freed up space elsewhere for passengers and luggage. In fact, there was so much space under the steeply raked bonnet that the spare wheel went in there, too.

The 1.2-litre L and TL models all came with a back seat that could be folded or removed completely, turning it into a cavernous semi-van. The headlining was quilted – quite eye-catching, that.

The torsion bar suspension made this a roly-poly car in corners, although it was perfectly safe, and its steel safety cage body structure was quite advanced. It was just a shame about the carburettors, which had an annoying habit of clogging up so the engine wouldn't start on cold mornings. And the daft positioning of the temperature gauge behind the gearlever meant that a boiled-over engine stranded a few owners. But Renault sold just shy of 1 million of them before replacing it with the 9 in 1983.

An engine mounted near-flat meant the spare wheel could go under the 14's bonnet, freeing up space in the cavernous cargo area.

WHAT THEY SAID AT THE TIME

'Very roomy in relation to compact exterior dimensions. Excellent seats and ride, versatile loading arrangements with rear door. Moderate performance but reasonable economy, and a competitive price for what it offers.' – *Autocar* magazine in March 1977 on the £2,662 14TL.

Rover 3500 SDl, 1976

British Leyland's track record for successful new car launches was a patchy one throughout the first half of the 1970s. One after another, they just seemed to miss the mark for a variety of reasons. The Rover 3500, however, was different. For one thing it had the design team of the Range Rover behind it, and for another it looked rather like a Ferrari.

After British Leyland was nationalised in 1974, the government sanctioned the cash needed to complete the 3500, whose SD1 codename implied that it was the first new car from the Specialist Division. It also guaranteed the finance to build a big new plant at Solihull in which to make the car.

The last all-new Rover saloon, the 1963 P6, had been a complex machine, with its Citroën-inspired separate base structure, unstressed bolt-on panels, and racing car-type De Dion rear suspension. It

'The Rover 3500 is a serious challenger to the executive cars of Europe on the grounds of performance, roadworthiness, space and comfort. Power steering, brakes, handling and ride excellent.' – *Autocar* magazine in November 1976 on the £4,974 3500 Automatic.

Rover copied the Ferrari Daytona for the visage of its much-anticipated 3500 in 1976 – a car that every schoolboy would have loved his dad to own.

was cutting-edge stuff, although research proved that technology for technology's sake didn't impress owners. They were more concerned about how the car performed every day, and one of the SD1's main tenets was to be simpler but no less of a performer.

So it had a conventional structure and a live rear axle, with a huge amount of effort poured into refining that format, aided by the smooth and powerful 3.5-litre Rover all-aluminium V8 engine, a brand-new five-speed gearbox and superb power steering.

Its fastback styling was the height of modernity, with a slick frontal treatment paying homage to the Ferrari Daytona, and an overall profile inspired by Pininfarina's acclaimed BMC 1800 concept car of 1968. The interior was a haven of crushed velour, with fresh air funnelled to the driver through a steering column vent and all the instrumentation contained in a futuristic-looking, boxy module mounted on top of the dashboard itself. If your dad could afford a car of this stature, then a Rover 3500 it just had to be.

The SD1's interior looked like something from TV's *Space 1999*; the instrument box could easily be switched for left-hand-drive manufacture.

WHO LOVED iT?

The awards came thick and fast, including European Car of the Year 1976, while designers like Spen King and David Bache were bestowed with Midlander of the Year medals for the prestige they brought to Solihull with the SD1. Just a pity, then, that the strike-bound British Leyland's build quality was quickly revealed to be lousy, despite the basic soundness of the handsome, composed car itself.

Volvo 343, 1976

The surprising thing about this small Volvo was how it seemed to get more popular the older it got, and with a production span for the expanded range lasting some fifteen years, that meant it was a very successful car for Volvo. Indeed, in 1982, '83 and '94 the 340/360 Series featured in Britain's Top 10 bestsellers' list.

Back in February 1976, this motoring phenomenon kicked off with a single model, the 343. Although badged as a Volvo, the car had been conceived by Netherlands-based DAF, whose car-making operation had been taken over by the Swedes in 1975. The DAF-designed compact three-door hatchback gave Volvo a ready-made entrant into the

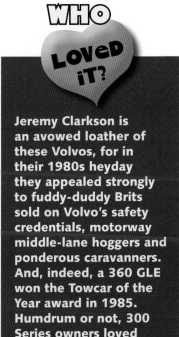

WHO LOVED iT?

Jeremy Clarkson is an avowed loather of these Volvos, for in their 1980s heyday they appealed strongly to fuddy-duddy Brits sold on Volvo's safety credentials, motorway middle-lane hoggers and ponderous caravanners. And, indeed, a 360 GLE won the Towcar of the Year award in 1985. Humdrum or not, 300 Series owners loved these solid, reliable cars.

This is a 1981 model of the Volvo 343, by then called the 340 Series and increasing in popularity year by year.

The plain 340 on the right was joined by the sparkling 360 GLT on the left after some clever Volvo cross-fertilisation of engines.

Golf-class family car sector. But it had several quirky features.

The main one was that DAF's variomatic constantly variable automatic system was the sole transmission offered. Another was that, in DAF tradition, this was installed at the back, above the De Dion tube-type rear axle that drove the rear wheels. The 70bhp 1.4-litre engine was supplied by Renault.

Once production was under way – helping Volvo grab a bigger share of the car market in the EEC, where Sweden was not yet a member – the company quickly got to work on expanding the appeal of this otherwise idiosyncratic car. By 1979, you could get one with manual transmission, five doors (the 345) and typical Volvo seats featuring open-centre head restraints. The fact was, the more Volvo-ised it became, the more people liked it, and the well-balanced, rear-wheel-drive layout very much suited a 2-litre Volvo engine option added in 1980. In 1982 this was offered in 115bhp fuel-injected form in the GLT model, a surprisingly capable little sports saloon; young chaps buy them today for peanuts for their abilities to be driven for rear-wheel-drive kicks.

WHAT THEY SAID AT THE TIME 'What, then, does this Volvo offer? Not performance, not economy, not looks, but the appeal of a new and interesting car with promise of safety and long life, and ease of driving with the CVT transmission.' – *Autocar* magazine in February 1977 on the £3,527 343.

Skoda Estelle, 1976

It is rumoured, but not substantiated, that Skoda was banned by Soviet Union diktat from making a modern, front-engined car, and that's why the new 105/120 Series introduced in 1976 stuck closely to the formula of the outgoing S100/110. That is, with four-cylinder engines slung out the back beyond the rear wheels and suspended by swing axles. In the Porsche 911, driven by experienced enthusiasts, a similar but refined set-up gives great handling, but in the little Skoda a manoeuvring blunder could lead to oversteer and the car in a ditch or a greengrocer's window.

In practice this rarely happened, because Skoda drivers tended to be cautious, with an eye to economy rather than recklessness. When in 1993 Skoda GB finally recalled its cars to have a look at the suspension, it criticised the Consumers' Association for 'sensationalising' a possible defect. There was no doubt, however, that the car could be troublesomely tail-happy if conditions got slippery.

There was quite a decent amount of luggage capacity under the unusual, side-opening bonnet … or else it was the best crumple zone in the world!

The new generation Skoda range in 1976, with the 120 on the left and the 105 on the right. They were reasonably neat lookers, but still rear-engined.

This controversy is where all the legendary Skoda jokes come from. Yet the cars were very popular. There was a choice of 44bhp 1046cc or 49–54bhp 1174cc engines (later, with a stylistic revamp in 1984, came a bigger 1289cc motor) with a four-speed gearbox. The petrol tank was under the back seat but the radiator was mounted at the front … so a black plastic radiator grille on the nose could legitimately be fitted! Luggage could be packed under the bonnet that, unusually, opened sideways. The Estelle name was adopted specially for the UK imports that began in 1977. The cars' spaciousness, reliability, easy DIY maintenance and, of course, absurdly low prices were all part of an appealing package that was no joke at all to those who opted for it.

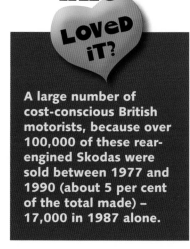

WHO LOVED iT?

A large number of cost-conscious British motorists, because over 100,000 of these rear-engined Skodas were sold between 1977 and 1990 (about 5 per cent of the total made) – 17,000 in 1987 alone.

The Estelle 120 GLS was Skoda's meek attempt at a little extra luxury, with a more dignified grille and large headrests.

Chrysler Sunbeam, 1977

It wasn't obvious to potential buyers perusing this neat little hatchback in Chrysler showrooms in 1977, but the Sunbeam had been funded by the Labour government. America's Chrysler, embattled proprietor of the old Rootes Group business, told ministers it was unfair to pour public money into British Leyland when Chrysler's own plant near Glasgow wasn't economically viable either. If they didn't get help, they might face closure.

The result, eventually, was a £55 million grant in 1975, but with some strings attached: first, a new car had to be created to build at Linwood, Scotland, in double-quick time; and secondly, every last scrap of it had to be British-sourced. That's how the Sunbeam came to be created in a breakneck nineteen months. And for a rush job, it wasn't bad at all.

The centre section of the car was identical to the Hillman/Chrysler Avenger, including the doors, but there was a neat, boxy front end and a shortened rear, with a large opening rear window doubling as a simple hatchback, albeit with a very high sill. The engine line-up included 1.3- and 1.6-litre Avenger units and also the thrifty 928cc aluminium engine formerly used in the Hillman Imp. Like the Avenger, it was rear-wheel drive; funds ran to nothing more modern. The steering wheel and instruments were borrowed from the recent Alpine.

Chrysler's clever reworking of the Avenger, along with British government funding, produced the Sunbeam in double-quick time.

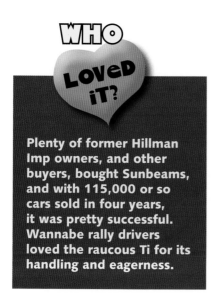

Plenty of former Hillman Imp owners, and other buyers, bought Sunbeams, and with 115,000 or so cars sold in four years, it was pretty successful. Wannabe rally drivers loved the raucous Ti for its handling and eagerness.

Not quite a true hatchback, the Sunbeam's large opening rear screen still made this a very useful car for shopping and hobbies.

You could have it as a basic LS, a GL, or the top-line GLS with a vinyl roof, and in 1979 there was a twin-carburettor, 100bhp Ti performance model and also the legendary 150bhp Sunbeam Lotus, which proved to be such an adept competition car it scooped the 1981 Manufacturers' World Rally Championship. By 1979, though, Chrysler UK had been sold to Peugeot and the new Talbot marque name was adopted. The Sunbeam lasted two more years until the French finally and unsentimentally shut Linwood down.

WHAT THEY SAID AT THE TIME

'The dynamic failings of the small-engined car aside, if the standard of trim and equipment on this basic LS is anything to judge by, then the more fully appointed cars will be to a very high standard. Some handling and braking limitations, also only a moderate ride.' – *Autocar* magazine in December 1977 on the £2,324 Sunbeam 1.0LS.

Matra Rancho, 1977

The dual-purpose Range Rover, naturally, was one of the most desirable cars around in the 1970s, rumbling through the more moneyed parts of Britain, both urban and rural, and it remains so in its fourth incarnation today. The major downer for most was the price, not to mention the colossal running costs. It took obscure but imaginative French company Matra to devise something that could plug the significant gap in the market, and the Rancho was the result.

People envied the Range Rover's versatility, high-riding stance and spirit of adventure; four-wheel drive was exciting, but not really necessary. So Matra based its design on the front-wheel-drive Simca 1100 pick-up, boosting the performance by fitting a 1.5-litre Alpine engine instead of the little Simca's 1.1-litre lump. At the back it built a steel-framed extension to the passenger compartment, stepping up the roofline so that the rear passenger seats could be positioned 10cm above the front ones for a panoramic view out.

There were huge side windows, a rear tailgate split into glass upper and glass-fibre lower sections just like the Range Rover, and a black plastic roof rack above the front passenger seats added luggage capacity and hid the join between the steel panels at the front and the plastic ones at the back. A chunky black plastic grille, side mouldings and wheel arches gave a cool and rugged appearance all round, and two large spot lamps just ahead of the windscreen fuelled the 'explorer' image.

It was, of course, all show with not much off-road go, unveiled in May 1977 and arriving in the UK exactly a year later. Ground clearance was quite limited and there was a sump guard to protect the engine if you foolishly attempted ploughing along deeply rutted tracks. But the Rancho made a great family fun car, especially after two extra seats for children were offered in the cavernous boot space … and it cost half the Range Rover's price. It was the groundbreaking ancestor of today's 'crossover' cars like the Nissan Qashqai and Ford Kuga.

A clever design by Matra created a cut-price Range Rover-type vehicle with a style all of its own and plenty of passenger space.

Anyone who yearned for a Range Rover but didn't have the necessary wonga. Even the most basic Land Rover cost 20 per cent more – and that was a thirsty boneshaker of an everyday car. With 58,000 Ranchos sold through the Chrysler and Talbot dealer network until 1985, sales massively outstripped the initial projection of 20,000.

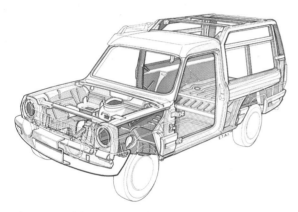

This structural drawing shows how the metal Simca pick-up cab was artfully grafted to Matra's glass-fibre rear compartment.

Later Ranchos were available with two extra seats, although they were rearward-facing and designed for children, so not great for a late-night homeward journey with tired little ones.

WHAT THEY SAID AT THE TIME

'For rough going it copes extremely well, since the suspension has ample travel and damping, and there is good ground clearance. It is just on the matter of hill-climbing and traction that it falls down. These things apart, it is still very versatile.'
– *Autocar* magazine in July 1978 on the £5,650 Rancho.

Fiat Strada, 1978

A huge amount of effort, and a vast amount of money, was sunk into the Fiat Ritmo project in an attempt to take on the Volkswagen Golf. Certainly, it looked like nothing else thanks to designers at Bertone, with its piggy-eyed headlights peering out from a substantial grey-plastic nose cone that could withstand 4mph bumps, circular door handles, and weird offset bonnet scoop, radiator grille, and even wheel trim designs. The interior was austere and modern, a festival of 1970s plastics.

The three- and five-door hatchbacks – launched in 1978 and UK-available in 1979, where it was renamed the Fiat Strada – made extensive use of existing Fiat 128 mechanical hardware, including the overhead-camshaft 1.1-, 1.3- and 1.5-litre engines derived from it. In 1980 came a 1.7-litre diesel, but all Stradas felt underpowered until the arrival of the peppy, twin-cam 105TC in 1981, which with 105bhp had twice as much power as a 1.1-litre car. Much later, and after a major revamp had calmed down the Strada's outlandish looks, the potent, twin-carburettor, 128bhp 130TC Abarth model was added. This version could sprint to 82mph from standstill in 7.8 seconds, and roar on up to 121mph. There was also a good-looking, but rarely seen, Cabriolet.

The British public were well aware of the Strada's arrival, thanks to a memorable TV advertising campaign entitled 'Handbuilt By Robots', shot by director Hugh 'Chariots of

In either three- or five-door forms, the Ritmo/Strada was an arresting-looking car, pitched fair and square at the Golf market.

Fire' Hudson to a stirring arrangement of Rossini's *Figaro*. It captured the Strada's highly automated production process in spectacular fashion. The car was capable, good to drive and roomy, and yet the older Golf remained a better car. The Strada's many merits were further overshadowed in Britain by poor reliability and an almost instant reputation for rust.

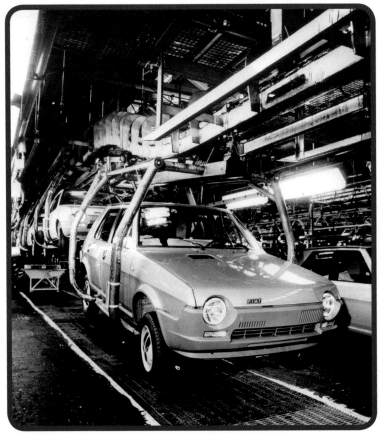

A freshly minted Ritmo/Strada at Fiat's Turin plant. British TV viewers got to see the factory's robots in spectacular action in a memorable Hugh Hudson-shot commercial.

The Strada's launch had an enormous impact, and UK sales were initially brisk. But then the Ford Escort MkIII and the first Vauxhall Astra arrived; the Strada's moment soon passed and its reputation for fragility rapidly made it a no-no for canny buyers.

Into the 1980s

You may wonder why our review of 1970s cars peters out at 1978 with the Fiat Strada. The reason is that the final two years of this period were an unusually quiet and uneventful time for new model launches. Almost all the unveilings were of minor additional models, facelifted versions, or else relatively insignificant cars – Audi 200, Daihatsu Charade, FSO Polonez, Toyota Starlet – that proved only passing irritants to top-selling rivals. Even the introduction of the Vauxhall Carlton executive car in 1978 was a curiously underwhelming event, and it singularly failed to tempt customers away from the Ford Granada that they liked so much.

But we also wanted to keep the flavour of our story firmly rooted in what we can all recall from life on the road in Britain in this decade. For example, the Lancia Delta, Peugeot 505, Renault 18 and Saab 900 all arrived on our shores in 1979, but by the time we saw decent numbers of them around the place, the 1980s had dawned. And although the stylish, rotary-engined RX-7 was to be found in one or two Mazda dealers' showrooms by the end of 1978, it would always remain a rare sight.

However, towards the end of 1979 there came two car launches that were highly significant. The first was the debut of the majestic and highly acclaimed Mercedes-Benz S-Class at the Frankfurt Motor Show. It positively bristled with new

▲ Ford's third-generation Escort of 1980 was as radical as it was attractive, with a brand-new range of transverse engines driving the front wheels, and the zesty XR3 as the new performance iteration.

▼ This ghosted image shows the complex inner workings of the Lancia Delta HF 4x4, a highly influential car that was a marvellous rally machine with Martini sponsorship.

safety features, such as the first anti-lock brakes and driver airbag as standard equipment on a mainstream production car; the design was handsome and aerodynamic, and engines ranged from a 3-litre straight-six to a 5-litre, all-aluminium

V8. It absolutely catapulted forward the benchmark large luxury cars needed to reach; the quality was amazing and so were the prices!

Also from Germany in 1979 was the other big new player, the Opel Kadett. Or, rather, it would become

▲ Although launched in 1978, the brilliant Saab 900 was a child of the 1980s, and helped establish the Swedish brand as a credible force in the premium car sector.

so when its Vauxhall-branded running mate, the Astra, was launched in early 1980. The Kadett/Astra followed the VW Golf package to the letter, with a transverse engine driving the front wheels, a roomy cabin, and a choice of three- and five-door hatchbacks.

Renault 14, Chrysler/Talbot Horizon, Vauxhall Astra – they all helped to stimulate intense competition around a very similar format of family car. And in Britain, at least, the Golf-Astra paradigm would receive its biggest broadside yet in the autumn of 1980

▲ This is the 1978 Mazda RX-7, a new dawn for the rotary engine and a much-admired sports coupé of the early 1980s period.

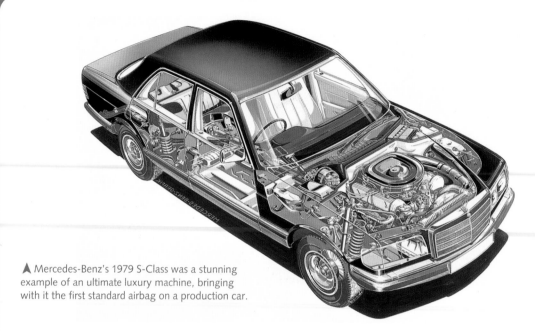

▲ Mercedes-Benz's 1979 S-Class was a stunning example of an ultimate luxury machine, bringing with it the first standard airbag on a production car.

when Ford pitched in with its closely matched Escort MkIII, an all-new car from its range of four-cylinder CVH engines and a neat, 'bustle-backed' tailgate.

In very much the same way, it was hard to slip a cigarette paper between the Renault 5, Fiat 127, VW Polo and Ford Fiesta in the supermini class. But the embattled British Leyland, dragged back from the brink of meltdown by Michael Edwardes and his capacity to stand up to the unions and shut loss-making plants, was able to get a decent shoe-in with the Austin Mini-Metro.

The fanfare surrounding the car was massive, as it carried the fortunes of the state-owned carmaker with it; it was simply too important to fail. And despite the limitations of having to reuse the Mini's A Series engines, four-speed gearbox and front subframe structure, the

Metro turned out to be a good effort indeed, notably roomy and, by British Leyland's lamentable recent standards, pretty well built thanks to a robot-heavy refit of the Longbridge, Birmingham factory.

So, by the time 1980 came to a close, the trendsetters for the ten years ahead were all out of the traps. The unfolding era of royal weddings, big hair, New Romantics, the CD player, Sloane Rangers and Yuppies, privatisations, aerobics, Ronald Reagan, nouvelle cuisine, the Filofax and Channel 4 was set to overturn much of the torpor and drudgery

▲ The 1980 S-Class's aerodynamics were fastidiously researched by Mercedes-Benz to give the stately car optimum wind resistance.

◄ It's November 1981 and the first Vauxhall Astra to be built on Merseyside comes off the line; up until then it had been an Opel-made import. The Opel Kadett/Vauxhall Astra certainly was a strong competitor to the Golf.

associated at the time with the previous decade, for good or for bad. Car-wise, it would be a time when small diesel engines rose rapidly in popularity for the relative cheapness of their fuel and the huge increases in economy they offered. Turbocharging and four-wheel drive would spread from high-performance cars to family models. A five-speed gearbox would gradually become a necessity rather than a sports car asset, while alloy wheels seemed to lose their scientific advantage in unsprung weight and became a shiny, trim level nicety, intrinsic, like fancy decals and a stereo-radio cassette, to the multitude of limited editions that all manufacturers indulged in. Japanese cars, meanwhile, keenly adopted the 'European look', and in 1982 we would see the first South Korean cars on British roads when Hyundai imports got off to a discreet start.

Disquiet about the environmental and health effects of exhaust pollution, especially from leaded

▲ Metros rolling off the Longbridge production line in 1980. They called it 'A British car to beat the world'. Hmm, not quite, but a sizeable success nonetheless.

petrol, would snowball during the '80s. Unleaded petrol went on sale for the first time in 1986 and within six years new cars would be routinely fitted with catalytic converters in their exhaust systems as the car industry began – literally – to clean up its act.

Well before all that, the wearing of front seatbelts finally became a legal requirement in 1983, and while that was certainly the biggest change to hit drivers inside their cars, probably the greatest change outside was the ability, from September 1986, to drive all the way around London and its sprawling outskirts on the completed M25. Margaret Thatcher opened it by snipping a ribbon

▲ The Austin Metro was launched to enormous fanfare in 1980, and it carried the entire fortunes of the embattled British Leyland with it. Fortunately, for a brief time, it did the trick.

▼ Cars from South Korea would not register on the British radar until 1982, when the first Hyundai Pony went on sale in a low-key launch at the Motor Show.

between Junctions 22 at London Colney and 23 at South Mimms.

At 117 miles long, it was the planet's longest orbital highway, and had taken thirteen years to complete from the first sod being dug at South Mimms to the final stretch of tarmac being rolled flat. It cost £909 million, around £7.5 million a mile. Rock guitarist Chris Rea was inspired by M25 traffic queues to write the title track of his 1989 album *The Road to Hell* … and not a lot has changed in the near thirty intervening years …

Left: The 1973 London Motor Show at Earl's Court –
where the Austin Allegro was a star attraction, alongside
the Morris Marina and Mini Clubman – still featured
traditional British marques with the biggest stands, and
drew a huge crowd, but it would be downhill all the
way for British Leyland from this point on.

Above: Audi was small fry in Britain when this image of the
combined 1971 Audi and NSU range was taken. The upmarket
Audi 100 (front, right) and 100 Coupé (centre) were signs of the
great things to come from the Volkswagen-owned marque in the
future. Sadly, though, the wonderful Ro80 (front, left) would be
the end of NSU and its ambitious rotary-engined odyssey.

OTHER TITLES PUBLISHED BY
THE HISTORY PRESS

100 Cars Britain Can Be Proud Of
Giles Chapman
978-0-7524-5686-7

Bizarre Cars
Keith Ray
978-0-7524-8771-7

Visit our website and discover thousands of other History Press books.
www.thehistorypress.co.uk